Queen of the Fall

AMERICAN LIVES | SERIES EDITOR: TOBIAS WOLFF

Queen of the Fall

A MEMOIR OF

GIRLS & GODDESSES

SONJA LIVINGSTON

University of Nebraska Press | *Lincoln and London*

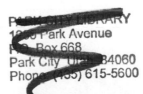

Set in Garamond Premier Pro by Rachel Gould.

This is a work of literary nonfiction based on memory,
perception, and personal experience. Some names and
identifying information have been changed to respect
the privacy of others.

For my mothers, actual and acquired
and
In memory of Judith Kitchen

Contents

Queen of the Fall

Introduction

The Memory of Trees

WE BEGIN WITH APPLE trees. An orchard at harvest time: trees wild with growth, branches pushing into sky the color of oceans on classroom globes, blue like swimming pools and certain perfect crayons. I start up a ladder set against a tree—how else to reach the red circles of fruit? But I can go only so high. The bigger kids might catch glimpses of Lake Ontario climbing as they do. They might see past the lake and into Canada even, but I switch between the lowest rung and the ground, watching my brothers and sisters pick apples and return to earth in scurries and jumps. They call out for me to come and catch whatever shakes loose from the tree, laughing and talking, making claims over who has the most and everyone wins because you have never seen so much fruit and so many hands reaching for it.

It's like a trip to the zoo, this place of tree and sky and my family scaling together the branches.

We have our good times, loading into the station wagon and driving to the Orleans County Fair. We travel to the center of town to see the parades down on Main Street, lining up on sidewalks, pressing our knees into Vs as we make seats of the curb, lifting our hands to direct the marching band, following the crash of tuba, cymbal, and snare. Once or twice a year our eyes go fat as moons as the majorettes pass, the flash of baton and the tap of shoes, the scrambling for candy tossed by beauty queens from flatbeds and slow-moving convertibles. We know about sparklers and the Fourth of July. We understand picnics and firecrackers and heat lightning, yes. There are birthday cakes and trick or treat and even Christmas morning, but nothing like this day: the air crisp and clean, the trees letting us into their crowns, the apples coming as they do, a shower of valentines falling into open hands.

The apple is the trickiest of fruits. It's what did Eve in, they say. All that unbridled longing and the foolishness of allowing herself to be sweet-talked by a snake. She caved, and in doing so, became a sort of red fruit herself, maybe even a snake. Either way, Eve was emblematic as she wrapped her arms around Adam and became the source of his collapse. Snake. Eve. Adam. The order of wrongdoing. But what can be expected of a snake? What can be expected of a man, especially where a woman is concerned? So it was Eve, really, who shouldered the blame. Her shoulders were strong, at least, maybe as broad as Adam's, for it's said she was fashioned from one of his ribs. How odd to imagine woman made from man when everyone knows it's the woman who bears fruit, the whole of her body bending to the task, ribs and elbows and knees working to support her growing belly. But the Bible gives us Eve with her long hair and borrowed rib resting a hand against the tree she's already been considering as the snake winds round the trunk, all slippery skin and big talk.

I wonder if Eve came to regret it, the fruit. It's implied, of course, because she saw right away her nakedness and covered herself with leaves. But hiding is shame, not sorrow, and what is fruit if not meant to be eaten? Where would the story be if they'd linked arms and walked right on by that glorious tree? So they fell. So they had to pack up and leave Paradise. But how much more they had to say to each other then, how much wider the world and how lasting the memory of the tree—during even the hardest of times, there would be the taste of it, brave upon their tongues.

I say to my sister when we're older, *Do you remember that time in Albion with the apple trees?* I describe the lake, which I could not have seen so much as felt shimmering just beyond the orchard. *Apple trees everywhere*, I say, *all of us reaching for fruit, the blue sky and perfect clouds.* I see her as the dark-haired girl she was pushing into the branches, and think of the names of old-fashioned varieties (Winesap, Northern Spy, Queen of the Fall), swooning the way one does over long-gone days until she breaks in, *You mean the time Ma signed us up to work as migrants?*

We laugh then, because what else can you do when memory is cracked wide enough to include the reality of day labor? How different my sister's recollection, how costly sometimes knowledge. Her account must be technically correct. There was never enough money. My mother did not fear hard work, enjoyed being outdoors, and would have thought it a wonderful opportunity, a day or two of picking together in the field. It's possible someone shouted orders, saying, *Come on now, the day's half done*, shooting dirty looks at my mother and her children hanging like monkeys from trees. Perhaps we were paid by the bushel. It's likely, of course. But my impression does not catch up so quickly and the only green I remember is the press of leaves cloaking the shyest apples.

How fickle it is, memory—preferring some days to others, granting first a blue sky, offering next the sound of laughter, swelling our remembrances until a largeness seeps into the grain of things and memory itself becomes billowed and flapping. The way it renders its stories without the burden of fact. The fact is that even with so many children, there was no father to be found. The fact is that the lot of us must have looked so ragged we inspired pity in all who passed. The fact is that we were probably in the orchard as laborers. Those are facts but not the truth, which does not even speak the same language. My sister's information adds a new layer to the scene—providing another lens through which to view the apple trees, explaining the circumstances of the day perhaps, widening the scope, to make us laugh and shake our heads as slivers of shame threaten to seep into the orchard—but making it does nothing to memory itself, which does not change, cannot change, and remains as it was to a girl too young to understand picking apples for anything other than pleasure.

Come now and let us return once again to the branches, close enough to see the child standing beside a ladder, a girl in old corduroys and flat red sneakers whose neck is sore from so much looking up as she races to catch falling fruit and tries hard to fill her basket.

I

This is how easily the pit opens.
This is how one foot sinks into the ground.

RITA DOVE, "Persephone, Falling"

Land of the Lost

SHE'S THE GIRL EVERY other girl wants to be. Ivory skin. Feathered hair. A tiny mole orbiting her crooked smile, a smile that puts one in mind of Kristy McNichol, the actress who plays Buddy on TV's *Family*, whose cuteness is like new kittens, who breaks America's heart open each and every time they tune into the show. It's 1979. Skin that tans, a decent pair of Candie's shoes, and a Kristy McNichol smile are everything. But there's something else. Leah, who has these things and could rule over other girls on the street, does not hold court. She speaks in whispers as she tucks filmy cotton blouses into faded Levi's and wraps braided leather belts around her tiny waist—not knowing how much it hurts other girls not to have the creamy skin, the impossibly small waist. Leah Fiuma does not know the weight of such things and though her shyness sometimes comes off as indifference, her prettiness is sometimes mistaken for superiority; in truth, Leah doles out kindness where other girls might dole out pain.

"Don't tell anyone," she says as we make our way up the stairs and into her room, past the *Breaking Away* movie poster taped to her wall. Leah's vanity sits beneath the poster of a blond boy on his bicycle and includes a cushioned bench and pivoting mirror. It's been repainted many times, some of the old color showing through where it has chipped, but still, it's a vanity, and Leah may as well be Miss America, because besides the dressing table, she has a red handkerchief blouse trimmed in lace with butterfly sleeves that flutter about the arms. Leah has let me borrow this blouse on precisely two occasions, and as I follow her into her room, I can't help but hope that the subject of the blouse will come up again—that she will offer, that I will accept.

Leah Fiuma rarely invites other girls into her room, and when she does, it's mainly to talk about the boy she loves, the one everyone knows is wrong—the one Amberlee Mangione has nicknamed Sleestak.

Sleestaks are reptilian creatures from *Land of the Lost*, a Saturday morning TV show in which the Marshall family has slipped through a time portal and become trapped in an alternate universe inhabited by sleestaks and dinosaurs and even the mythological Medusa living in a garden of stone. They struggle to survive, the strong-jawed Rick Marshall and his kids, Will and Holly, exploring their new world, escaping the various monsters and traps, while trying to make it back home.

Back in our world, Amberlee struggles to understand how the prettiest girl on the street could succumb to a boy so ugly. Sleestak's blue-black hair drips like oil onto skin that rises in swollen pink foothills across an expanse of forehead and cheek. Though Leah uses it in every other sentence, I fail to retain Sleestak's actual name. And it doesn't matter. Not really. The main point is her choosing me to tell about him. She's done it before, asked me to her room. Just a few times, but enough so that I stand taller as I follow her onto the front porch, snaking through a clump of her brothers who smoke weed to the sounds of Crosby, Stills, and Nash.

I'd like to think that Leah asked me up here because I'm one of the few who doesn't judge her for loving Sleestak, but it's probably because I'm not technically in sixth grade until September and am too young to formulate meaningful judgment. And what do I care for reasons when I'm occasionally rewarded with a curlicue of pink blush and the chance for close-up observation of the proper way to brush back one's bangs? Boys seem years away, but liquid blusher and the secrets of feathered hair—these are mysteries in need of immediate unraveling.

"Don't tell anyone," she says again. "Especially not your mother."

Such caution makes me wonder if she's going to talk about something other than Sleestak today. Leah stands at the window overlooking our dead-end street, pulling the white cotton curtains closed while I fumble with my fingers, sensing the importance of a secret requiring the drawing of curtains and worrying whether I'm an adequate choice for such disclosure. But she doesn't seem concerned as she walks to the vanity. She must have a new shade of eye shadow or is about to explain the mechanics of the eyelash curler whose metal bends intrigue me. The girls in my family don't wear makeup; my mother forbids it. But I've seen the tools of beauty in the homes of friends, and always, I watch, waiting for secrets to unfold.

Leah fishes through the small drawer, pushing things around, until finally, she emerges with a trifold brochure and I try not to show my disappointment while wondering if she's planning to tell me something academic. She's older, in high school—another universe practically— and who knows, maybe brochures are a part of it all. She sits beside me, the chenille dots of her bedspread imprinting the backs of our legs as she opens the brochure and sets it onto our knees, revealing photographs that look blistered and scarlet.

"Can you see them?" Leah's eyes are like the Sacred Heart of Jesus print every mother on the street has hanging in her living room. All the Fiumas have those eyes—baby blue made lighter by sand-colored skin. Because it's summer and the sun has bronzed her face, Leah's eyes are little flames.

"See what?" I ask. All I see are glossy piles of red. Words crowd the spaces surrounding the photographs, but with her watching I can't read quickly enough to understand. Only the way she holds her breath makes meaning for me.

"Babies," she whispers. Her Jesus eyes turn toward the brochure, looking as if the weight of every bad thing has settled onto her shoulders. "Some girls get pregnant and do this to their babies."

I have always been an unfortunate combination of knowing and painfully unaware. For as far back as I can remember, I was a sponge for what fell from people's mouths. I loved words and was never disappointed because more than any other thing, the world is filled with words. Some, like *saturation* and *photosynthesis*, came from school, while others, like *jive-ass* and *pimp-walk*, came from the streets. They swam about my head, such words, but even as I aced the weekly vocabulary tests at school, I was technically impaired—understanding nothing of the architecture of an apology, for instance, or how to tie a slip knot or the mechanics of the sexual interactions we joked about so freely in the cafeteria, so that even with the photographs laid out before me, I could make no sense of what I saw.

No, I didn't understand what I saw, but I looked hard anyway and the images stayed with me, the soft carnage of them. And the image of Leah Fiuma stayed with me as well. Leah with the hovering mole, thinking of her boyfriend perhaps and many other things as she stared into the brochure and said, "Isn't it terrible?"

The word, of course, was *abortion*, and once it came from her mouth, I received it and held it to me the way I'd held other words; some, like *marzipan* and *malarkey*, caused ridiculous joy, while others, like *phlegm* and *masticate*, I wished I'd never heard because of the way certain words refuse to leave once they wrangle their way inside. And after she gave it to me, the new word, I stored it away, recognizing it when it came a few years later, in health class, when we were assigned to write papers telling what we thought—whether abortion was right or wrong. What could I possibly have written? In a neighborhood with the highest rate of teen pregnancy in a city with the highest rate in the state, all of us with sisters or friends whose laps had been overtaken by babies—what did that teacher of ninth-grade girls really expect us to say?

I want to be as heartbroken as Leah as we look into the brochure. We move to the window when I admit I can't see anything and she thinks maybe some light will help. I try, but can't make out what she's waiting for me to see. After a few attempts at pointing out tiny fingernails, I finally pretend to recognize them while stealing peeks at the vanity, wondering when she'll fold away the brochure, take up her pearly pink lip gloss and tell me one more time the way Sleestak has become her world.

Whatever happened to that brochure? That chipped vanity? The poster of a boy on a bicycle pushing into the wind? Soon after that visit, Leah went into hiding with Sleestak, who was running from the police over problems with drugs. She had a baby not long afterward and—who knows?—maybe a couple more. Her mother was a cashier at a local university and Leah and her brothers could have gone to college for free—a fact much touted in a neighborhood where ringing up lunches was the closest anyone got to college. And though I don't think any of the kids ever made use of their mother's tuition benefit, it was practically a law degree on our street, Mary Fiuma's tuition waiver, the way it impressed. Now such things hardly matter. A breeze coming up from the past, that tuition benefit, nothing more than the flutter of a page.

I keep my promise to Leah and don't tell my mother the word she's taught me, never once mentioning the brochure. Not because I'm especially good at secrets, but because this one has no weight. A new ankle bracelet would have pressed heavier against me. A silver bloom of hair spray. The word does not rise in me for many years and when it finally does, it involves the case of a sister. She's young, still in high school, so I will take her for the procedure, I tell my mother. Planned

Parenthood will help schedule and pay, I let her know, because if there's one thing none of us has, it's money. But no. My mother says no. *We don't believe in abortion*, she says, and I shake my head and wonder what we do believe in. The edges of the Sacred Heart of Jesus have worn thin. Leah is long gone, and taken with her that vanity full of secrets. What then, I wonder, what then?

Last I heard, Leah was dancing at the Barrel of Dolls, a strip club near the railroad tracks, the place across the street from a figure drawing studio where men use charcoal to trace the lines of women hired to pose nude before them. They are men practicing art. Over at the Barrel, men make an art of sitting on barstools surrounded by the grind of beer and undulating women, using their eyes to capture the outlines of bodies, using their mouths to make color.

Maybe she's still there, spinning herself into middle age, though I think even Leah must be past pretty by now and anyway, I hope she has something gentle, after years of dollar bills being the thing to make her dance. Maybe Sleestak stayed by her side and grew respectable with the years. Maybe she left him for another man, someone who'd crossed over from the figure drawing studio and saw something still shimmering in her hair. Maybe her mother's tuition benefit waited for her, after all, and she took up painting herself and spends her days sitting in the sun with canvas and oil paint. Maybe something like magic happened in the case of Leah Fiuma. I don't believe much in magic, but I don't underestimate it either—not where such things as need and beauty are concerned.

And this is power of memory. This is what the mind can do, if you allow it to rise from its thick beams and dirt-packed basements, if you invite it to wander without tether, unnailed by the hammer of logic. It can go back thirty years to that dead-end street and find Leah as she was. Before the Barrel of Dolls. Before babies and the trifold brochure. I can find Leah Fiuma sitting once again before her vanity, butterfly blouse falling from her shoulders while she rubs a dab of pink into her cheeks. This is memory, yes, but something new has come to join it, a mystery larger than Jesus or Sleestak or anything contained in that brochure. The two of us sit once again beneath a poster of a boy on his bicycle pedaling into the wind, the sound of "Suite: Judy Blue Eyes" floating up from the front porch. It's 1979; I'm eleven years and perched on the edge of everything. I push my fingers through the raised patterns of the bedspread while roses open in Leah Fiuma's face, and for a moment, there's nothing ugly in the world.

Our Lady of the Lakes

HOW WE LONGED TO see her—hoping, even praying sometimes, for her to appear. But then our greed was nothing new, especially where groceries were concerned. On shopping days, a dozen hands pawed the insides of brown paper bags, touching the surface of things, blessing the potatoes with our longing, placing our palms upon cartons of eggs and bags of flour—those shopping days were like a holiday to a family of seven children. The oldest or most jaded among us might suck her teeth and make wisecracks about the abundance of generic labels and the same old sacks of rice, but it was merely posturing. The giddiness infected us all, brightened even the cracked linoleum floor and persisted beyond the unpacking of food, everything in the house temporarily overflowing. But even then, in the highness of those grocery days, it would have been tempting fate to expect her. It would have been wanting too much and foolish besides because my mother usually bought off-brand or—God forbid—margarine and we were, in fact, most often deprived of her.

Still, there were times when she'd appear in the bottom corner of a bag, hidden among canned corn or bags of puffed wheat, astonishing as a box of Pop Tarts, wondrous as name-brand sugar cereal. There she was, on a package of butter, an Indian maiden kneeling in the grass, the blue of lakes and sky converging behind her, accompanied by flowers and pine trees and sometimes cows.

The design of the box changed over time, but the maiden always wore a buckskin dress and beaded belt. Always, her hair was raven and lit with feathers. Always, she held a box of sweet cream butter in her hands, presenting it with such reverence that the very idea of butter became something of a religious offering.

With her fair skin and rosebud mouth, she didn't look like any Indian maiden we'd ever known—and we'd known plenty during our time on the reservation near Buffalo, women with golden skin and smiles ten times wider than the woman kneeling in the meadow. But who could be picky where butter boxes were concerned? Maidens were big in the 1970s, the culture helping itself to headbands and beadwork but feeling progressive because people had learned not to say *squaw*. Other than a fascination with Muhammad Ali, the Bermuda Triangle, and the general rise in the popularity of horror films, nothing marks my early childhood so much as the distorted affection for all things Native.

The package itself was an achievement for the way the maiden held in her hands a replica of the very same carton on which she appeared, so that the entire image—maiden and lake and pines—were repeated ad infinitum, the girl and her butter box continuing forever. But the endless loop of butter and maiden was simply an added bonus; the magic of recursive packaging, while captivating, was not why she mattered.

The real trick was her knees. The shine of the exposed caps, the gleam of them, the way they flashed flesh and reflected light in just the right places. And more than that, the way the perfect beads of her knees provided a secret revealed only to those wise in the ways of butter packaging.

Some used a razor to cut away a square surrounding her kneecaps, a small patch of cardboard which was lifted and pasted onto the maiden's chest. We were less brutal—not because we were kind, but because we were children with limited access to razors and too impatient to mess with scissors and glue.

We'd slip the sticks of butter from the box as soon as groceries were unloaded, erupting into fights over the cardboard panels, eventually divvying them between the siblings or cousins, taking turns folding the package the way we'd learned to do—bringing the maiden's knees up to her chest, transforming the exposed caps into a stunning pair of breasts, the polished divots looking for all the world like perfectly bronzed nipples.

You would have thought that the secrets of the universe were unfolded for how often we bent that carton back and forth. Hundreds of times, and as often as we could. Until the crease gave way and the bottom half broke off—the maiden's legs forever severed from the rest of her body. It *was* something like magic to witness the change from butter-bearing beauty to bare-breasted woman. There was a certain thrill in turning everyday body parts into the most private parts, and a real respect for the power of a few folds to render something as solid as butter packaging into low-grade pornography.

She was an object, Our Lady of the Lakes. But even as we coveted her image, my sisters and I knew better than to be impressed by such a Barbie doll version of a Native girl (or any girl). We must have questioned the reality of someone kneeling in greenery while happily offering up her dairy, and would eventually become disillusioned by the fact of women's bodies (ankles and faces and breasts) being used to sell products since the very idea of product came into being.

Still and all, I cannot help but think of her knees every time I pass her in the grocery cooler (how she knelt on them, what we did to them) where all these years later she still waits, stacked into tidy rows and smiling sweetly while holding out a box of butter—making offerings of herself for as far and as long as the eye can see.

The Lady with the Alligator Purse

IT HAPPENED LONG AGO, the thing that started me on this path. A fourth-grade play. We were to choose from a cast of historical figures and act as that person in our very own classroom production of *Famous Abolitionists of New York State* or *Forward-Thinking People of the Americas* or some such title. The first task was to select roles. The teacher lifted cardboard cutouts of various historical heads to show our options, until, one by one; we'd raised our hands to volunteer for a part. Frederick Douglass was snapped up in a second. As was Abraham Lincoln. Next went Harriet Tubman. Then Sojourner Truth. Even Dolly Madison was chosen before Susan B. Anthony—though how Dolly fitted into the play I fail to recall; perhaps the company that manufactured cardboard heads had sent our class an extra by mistake.

Who I played and how I managed to sneak past receipt of the pile of stiff fabric (crocheted shawl, wig, and lace collar) that was Susan B. escapes me. Was Vicky Marie Sweet, the girl who smelled of mothballs and pee, stuck being Susan? It's likely. I remember only their cardboard heads, the way Dolly Madison's name reminded me of fruit pies, and the tension seeping into the teacher's voice as she held Susan's unclaimed head: *Well, boys and girls, someone will have to be Miss Anthony.*

The view of Seneca Lake falls away as we eat but we talk easily, and the early passing of light is not such a loss. I'm getting to know this woman, a poet, and enjoying the dinner, not because of the food or the way the lake blackens before it disappears, but because of how her eyes rise from the twin circles of her glasses when I confess my interest in Susan B.

"Susan B. Anthony?" she says, and begins to describe one of the suffragist's acts in the next town over before starting in on her crab cakes. I nod. Western New York was a hotbed of religious and social upheaval in the nineteenth century, inhabited by the likes of Susan B. Anthony and Frederick Douglass in Rochester, Elizabeth Cady Stanton and Amelia Bloomer in Seneca Falls. Even today the region produces unexpected progressive bubbles in the midst of cabbage farms and Amish outcrops, so I'm not surprised to learn that Susan B. did something important in Waterloo, New York.

"What I'm most interested in," I say, "is whether the woman ever had any fun."

The poet goes silent for a moment, looking thoughtful while she chews, so that I'm afraid she's seen my comment as belittling of Susan B.'s lifetime of work on behalf of women. But no, she's not offended. She simply thinks and offers the slyest of smiles before speaking.

"I assure you, she had some fun." Her eyes rise above the glasses again as she sips water, "No need to worry about our Susan B."

Our Susan B.? She makes it sound like Susan is a friend, as if she's the woman walking into the restaurant this very moment to join us, waving and smoothing back blonde waves as she slips out of her coat. Every image I've ever seen of Susan B. floats before my eyes. All of them streaked gray. No hint the woman ever cracked a smile.

"How do you know?" I ask. "How can you possibly know?"

I like this woman for many reasons, her poetry and her humor, but most of all because my desperation to unearth the pleasures of a long-dead suffragist causes her no marked concern.

"Trust me," she says while fishing into her purse for a square of holistic gum. "Miss Susan had herself some good times."

Miss LuLu had a baby, she called him Tiny Tim,
She put him in the bathtub to see if he could swim.

"The Lady with the Alligator Purse": a thing to sing while clapping hands and jumping rope. A song in the same vein as "Miss Mary Mack" and "Have You Ever, Ever, Ever in Your Long-Legged Life?"

He drank up all the water, he ate up all the soap,
He tried to eat the bathtub, but it wouldn't go down his throat.
Call for the doctor, call for the nurse,
Call for the Lady with the Alligator Purse!

What child lights into a bathtub with his teeth? What mother lets him? Wholly nonsense. Holy nonsense. Such gobbledygook as only children can sing. I spent many hours inside the words of that song—my earliest memories involve listening as older girls sang and let their palms slap in quick rhythm, watching and waiting until I'd finally managed enough coordination of hand and mouth to join in.

So imagine my surprise, my utter surprise, to learn that Susan B. is the Lady with the Alligator Purse! The Susan B. Anthony House in Rochester even sells a replica of the oversized bag Anthony carried as she crisscrossed the country by wagon and train—a bag crammed with speeches and pamphlets and a copy of the transcript from the 1873 trial in which she was found guilty of the high crime of voting. She'd had it printed herself, that transcript, and insisted on showing it around.

In all the hundreds and thousands of miles she traveled speaking on behalf of women, even as the grown-ups shut her out, occasionally pelting her with harsh words and rotten fruit, children took note of her purposeful stride and that big old bag. Even if they had no inclination toward voting or the perusal of court transcripts, they noticed, and granted the woman in the high collar the honor of title role in their brilliant silliness.

It's late November. Roses still bloom in Memphis, but the weather has begun to change and the trees have finally started to let go of their leaves; the slender offerings of willow oak mainly, but fan-shaped leaves too, from ginkgoes gone gold all over the city. Each step along the sidewalk has me crunching on acorns with flesh the color of Tibetan monks' robes. And the smell of this walk, which rises from the combination of falling things and cool weather, reminds me of a man I once knew—something about the cherry tobacco from his pipe; more than the man himself, the inside of his mouth is something to remember. And I wonder as I trod upon scarlet magnolia seed and newly fallen leaves, did she ever know such things, Susan B., the taste of cherry smoke, the burning underside of autumn, the way such things can make a cathedral of the body?

Yes, the woman across from me says. *Yes.*

Back to the one eating crab cake while Seneca Lake fades from view. *Yes*, she says, winking as she says it, as if she understands the smoke and cathedrals folded into the question.

A well-known figure for most American schoolchildren, Susan B. Anthony was special where I grew up. Part of western New York State history, along with Douglass and his *North Star* and Tubman and the Underground Railroad with stations dotting the landscape—our own Lake Ontario, a crossing point to freedom. Such figures and their importance to the region were stamped into our heads. Names. Dates. Silhouettes.

But the things you said, Susan! The things you did!

If we were told of your chutzpah, I don't remember it. With your shawl and tight bun of hair, local hero or not, you were every girl's fear. And I think that you, dear Susan, or rather the image of you, the severe lines and hooded eyes, and the hair—my God, most of all the hair!—even as they held you out to us, you were made into a cautionary tale.

Voting itself is not the most riveting topic to fourth graders. Nor is it so riveting to adults perhaps, given the low turnout in elections. Who can say if we are rightly discouraged by the whole mess or whether we forget what it means to be denied the option. Even if the teacher had stirred us with impassioned testimony—the way the Nineteenth Amendment not only allowed women to vote but, in doing so, acknowledged them as human enough to be counted—even then, we still might have fought to be Frederick Douglass and Abraham Lincoln, leaving Susan B.'s head to hang heavy in her hands.

If only we'd known that she was the Lady with the Alligator Purse! If only we'd been told that she was the one we'd sung of since we first learned to sing, all the hand clapping and laughter, the rhyme itself becoming part of our bones, oh Susan, how the lot of us would have battled to be you.

"Perhaps it's a matter of marketing," I say to Sally, a friend with smart hair and smart thoughts, a woman, like me, who wants to not only admire but to cozy up to Susan B. Other friends—strong women, thoughtful women—admit to trying to relate to Ms. Anthony and finding themselves left cold.

I think of the Quakers, the group from which Susan sprung. Humanists and contemplatives, they are perhaps the most progressive of Christian sects, but are forever plagued by the image of the man on the side of the oatmeal box.

"Aren't they sort of like Amish?" a colleague once asked after I'd confessed attendance at Quaker Meeting. While I'd noticed a certain proclivity for natural fabrics and sensible footwear, there was not a pilgrim hat nor buckle shoe among the bunch. The Quakers, like their famous daughter, have a bit of an image problem. *No more laughing, no more fun—Quaker Meeting has begun.*

"We should scan an image of Susan and use Photoshop to loosen her up." I say to Sally. Erase that high collar. Unwind the bun, remove the fussy dress, and set her upon an oversized shell, like Aphrodite rising from the sea.

We laugh, imagining Susan B. in a white dress standing over a subway grate like Marilyn in *The Seven Year Itch*; or picturing her with earrings, a nose ring, and a *Love Hurts* tattoo. But the laughter goes only so far, no matter how we try to extend it, because we know what it means, the way we'd need to soften our best suffragist to make her a more popular American icon. As if the problem resided with the perfectly plain-faced Susan.

It's not a stretch to imagine that Susan B. ate all her vegetables.

I've heard talk of a ragdoll in her possession as a child, but the truth is that the Anthonys did not allow their children the distraction of toys so that they might better tune into the inner light, the higher plane. They wanted good things: freedom for slaves, opportunities for women—and my God, look at how they succeeded.

Still, I wonder about the vegetables and know somehow that little Susan B. made herself swallow her portion of stewed spinach. And this is where she loses me—though even this may be unfair. Maybe she spat them out while the other Anthonys were pondering educational reform. Perhaps little Susan looked toward the window and said, "Have you ever seen such a sunset?" and they, so unused to interruption from the dutiful daughter, would have had no choice but turn to the window while the dark-haired girl ran, mouth full of spinach, to the back of the house, emptying it into a stand of Queen Anne's lace.

"Tell me again how you like vegetables."

"I don't know," he says. "I just do."

He really does. My husband begins to twitch when green things are not included on a plate at a restaurant or in the home of a friend.

"But what part of you loves the kale—the part that knows it's good for you, or the spot on the tongue where flavor is sensed?"

"Both," he says, and I look at him sideways. May as well poke yourself in the eye with a stick. To willingly turn from something great tasting for something bitter but good for you demonstrates an uprightness not of my world, so that I begin to wonder if this penchant for pleasure is more my problem than Susan B.'s—who admittedly cares little either way. So why do I? Did she fear pleasure, or do I fear its opposite? The tight bun? Mouthful of greens? All backbone and resolution? What becomes of women without pink skin and soft smiles? What happens when I stop seeking out the sweet in every last thing?

Seriousness was a kind of rudeness where I come from.

Clarity of purpose was odd, follow-through was suspect, and planning was for people in other neighborhoods—those on TV and characters from books. Laughter first and laughter always. Even a face full of tears beat the hell out of tedium. But then, despite the larger culture, we seemed to escape much of the strict Protestant influence. *Idle hands are the devil's workshop*: I nearly choked the first time I heard that said. In the flickering lights of liberal Catholicism and the doctrine of poverty, there is no such thing as idle hands, no purpose greater than pleasure. To feel good *is* divine. Serious words come from others, those who think they know better. May as well go back to school for filmstrips on the metric system and the refrigeration plants of the Yucatán. No thanks and thank you very much. Pleasure first and pleasure last. Taste it now and taste it good, taste it all and taste it often, because life is nothing but one unpredictable surge—so use that mouth of yours to laugh and take wine and receive every last drop of every last thing because no one, and I mean no one, wants to suffer any of your straight talk.

Pleasure. The word itself is a sort of extravagance. The *s* and *u* coming together in a full-bodied rolling sound, the *x* in luxuriate, the oozing *z* of azure, the soul softening *d* in adieu. The Russians have a letter for this, the Ж, called *zheh*, the sound of lazy mornings an expanse of clean sheets, a sound with a certain *je ne sais quoi* as in the French *je*, but we of English tongue must make do, so that the sound becomes a combination of *s* and *u* and oh, what a word, rhyming with treasure— and if you say it the way the English do—even *leisure.* Swollen as the lushest *sh* as in hush and gush but deeper still, more resonant, as in resin, a sap of sorts, thick and viscous. *Pleasure.*

My feelings began to shift in sixth grade, in 1979, starting with the Susan B. Anthony dollar. They were smaller than the Kennedy coins my gambling grandmother had once won by the hundred and sent one per child back East, so that, to me, the Kennedy dollar was forever imbued with a kind of Vegas glitz. I'm not sure if Susan B. coins were ever placed in Vegas machines or whether such winnings would have been any less welcome by those cozied up to their slots, but even as a child I saw the way people disliked the Susan B. dollars. I'd never heard anyone talk about the faces on their money before and this dollar they spoke of as if someone had removed their wallets and replaced their coins with wafers of sawdust.

Despite the singsong slogan—*Carry Three for Susan B.!*—the Susan B. Anthony dollar was one of the most wildly unpopular coins in U.S. history.

Some took a rational approach to their dislike of the currency, complaining about its size and feel—too close to that of a quarter. But how much had to do with the face set into the metal? It was the first circulating American coin representing an actual woman and went largely unused. After sitting in treasury vaults by the millions, the Susan B. Anthony dollars finally found use in vending machines and mass transit fare boxes before being replaced by Sacagawea, whose Native face almost didn't make the cut when a poll indicated that the public preferred the allegorical image of the Statue of Liberty to the actual woman's face.

Still, I'm not sure that not wanting women on our money was the main problem. Evidence abounds to support the thought, of course, but I suspect that back in 1979, a Farrah Fawcett coin would have been more popular than Susan B.'s. Soft as a fawn, that Farrah, she might have become the most well-liked silver dollar in history. I could be wrong—a Farrah Fawcett dollar might have faltered as well. Money may be too serious for even the most pleasing of feminine forms. Perhaps we simply prefer our currency marked with a man's face.

Every woman should have a purse of her own.

Fifty years before Virginia Woolf prescribed a room for women, articulating the need for the space and money with which to create, Susan B. prescribed another space, one held close to the body, a container in which to hold private objects, which implied that a woman must first have private objects to hold. In her time, a married woman did not have her own money, her own bank account, or property. The husband owned all, decided all. And so Susan wanted for women a purse and something to put in it. Why do Susan B.'s words, said half a century before Virginia's, seem more difficult to swallow?

Money is power. Susan B. did not couch her speech behind niceties, and expected that others should do the same: *Forget conventionalisms; forget what the world thinks of you stepping out of your place, think your best thoughts, speak your best words, work your best works, looking to your own conscience for approval.*

She lobbied hard for the vote, pushed for reform that would enable women to keep their own pay, and campaigned for the admittance of women to the local university, but the leaving off of sugar in her words was perhaps Susan's most radical act. For a woman to talk of power without at least offering up a tray of cinnamon rolls—even now, such a woman might clear a room of all but the most devoted few.

Our job is not to make young women grateful, she said. *It is to make them ungrateful so they keep going. Gratitude never radicalized anybody.*

We do not take kindly to women who fail to modulate their tones, whose faces become misshapen through the firmness of their mouths, who risk unpleasantness. Which brings me to the Hillary Clinton nutcrackers for sale at Dulles Airport when she ran for president a few years back. How she was taken apart for the flat voice, the fixed mouth, the speaking plainly of her views. How groups fluttered around the nutcracker display, progressive-looking men and women strapped into mile-high heels. How fun it might be to buy a Hillary nutcracker for their friends.

What would she think of the Hillary nutcrackers, Susan B.? Once she got over the shock of air travel and prepackaged peanuts. Perhaps she'd sidle up to the bar, order a pint, and laugh over the Hillary nutcrackers as I could not.

But no. I don't suppose Susan would make use of the airport bar.

She worked for temperance after all—and while those women with their sashes are often portrayed as a band of harridans, what other power did they have? Wives lacked the ability to leave husbands and had no source of income to feed their children. Such women as Susan were less opposed to alcohol than in support of keeping money in husbands' pockets and preventing bruises that sometimes accompanied drunkenness as they came stumbling home. Most women of the era had to rely on prayers and hope, but those few who could afford to raised their voices and made themselves into beautiful nags.

By marriage, the husband and wife are one person in law: that is, the very being or legal existence of the woman is suspended during the marriage, or at least is incorporated and consolidated into that of the husband.

—BLACKSTONE'S LAW (1765)

And the way you did it, Susan. Striding into that barbershop and demanding to vote. Blackstone's Law had come to the colonies from England and a century later, still governed American thought on relations between men and women. The way you made them uncomfortable, standing tall as a man, demanding to be counted—Blackstone himself might have caved. The way you requested cuffs when they came for you on Thanksgiving Day, not settling for a quiet apology, the polite explanation—not with so much at stake. You put your arms out and insisted on cuffs. And the sham of your trial, the way they tried to squelch your voice. But you spoke. *You spoke.* When no one wanted to hear, you went against the very grain of what a woman should do; you refused to back down—standing when asked to sit, using your voice, and making the whole of the room uncomfortable.

You knew that women were as intelligent and feeling as men, knew it so keenly it became part of your body, which remained straight as you spent your days traveling hard miles only to be received with foul language and mocked in the papers, even burned in effigy. You shook it off and kept going, standing before a podium saying, *There shall never be another season of silence until women have the same rights men have on this green earth.*

You were at war. The dialogue may have been polite, the prisoners in cages they couldn't even see, but it was war nonetheless. Yes, I begin to see that such bearing as yours would have been the only possible thing.

"Help Me Make It through the Night": the song I'd sing with Susan B. if she ever came calling. I'd let her have the first line before chiming in, both of us singing about ribbons and shadows and the letting down of hair. We'd sing the Gladys Knight version because I can't imagine Susan would be much for the country-and-western original, which is fine because there's no wrong way to sing that song. We'd sit together, me in my jeans, Susan in her black dress and red shawl (the fourth-grade teacher had it wrong with her pile of gray; Susan's shawl was scarlet as the tip of a blackbird's wing!). We'd sit together singing our Gladys Knight song good and slow, taking our time with the words, trading verses and reaching for the high notes, until something inside each of us came loose.

"Mumps!" said the doctor.
"Measles!" said the nurse.
"Vote!!" said the Lady with the Alligator Purse.

Miss LuLu seems to have been most in need of parenting classes. But since she's a figure trapped in a hand-clapping song, let us sit back and watch as her baby locks onto a bathtub with a new row of nubby teeth. Let us listen as she calls in the medical professionals only to throw them out one at a time. Let us marvel that such a woman—when all is said and done—knew enough to trust you, Miss Susan.

Miss LuLu kicked the doctor;
Miss LuLu punched the nurse;
Miss LuLu paid the Lady with the Alligator Purse!

Gray hair, ashen face, ridiculed, and worse. But you, dear Susan, are the one for whom the song is named, yours is the song still sung by little girls, a playful chant, whose words we remember by heart.

My favorite place to walk is near you.

The Victorian cemetery at Mt. Hope. A pair of hydrangea trees grows nearby, whose flowers will have moved from cream to pink to rust by now. I pass the others too, Frederick Douglass and Adelaide

Crapsey and the handful of markers I visit for the pleasure of seeing their names set in stone. There's the giant basswood whose branches bend to the ground. How fine it feels to stand at the base and look up into the tumble of branches and leaves all light and shadow. But when I can delay no more, I go to you and stand for a minute by your stone, sometimes muttering a few words, leaving a wild violet or adding to the small pile of pebbles left by others who have come.

Oh, if I could but live another century and see the fruition of all the work for women! There is so much yet to be done.

—SUSAN B. ANTHONY

No matter what use we make of our days, they end. That is the sad fact of life. Despite your determination, your forward thrust and ramrod back, not even you, Susan, could live another hundred years. You lived to be eighty-six—long enough to plant seeds in the hardest of soils, but not long enough to taste the fruit. Not long enough to enjoy the streamers and the marching bands, not long enough to cast a vote without arrest.

It has been one hundred years, and what would you think of this world? What would you make of Kardashians and sexting and the soft scatter of our lives?

And what a silly woman you might find me, all this time spent imagining the spitting up of perfectly good spinach, picturing you as Aphrodite and Marilyn, singing about ribbons falling from our hair. You'd be right about how foolish I am in some ways, except that I am capable of reform. At least that's what I'd say once I talked you into my company, because I'd say anything to keep you near.

Come and settle into the seat at my side as we drive to Madison Street and your old house, then on to Mt. Hope to visit your people— your sisters and brothers and parents—and this is where, I'm sorry, Susan, but I'll have to drive north and ask if maybe we could to go up to the lake for a frozen custard, though I somehow know a furrowed brow would be your only reply, no matter how I go on about the custard, the sweet chocolate, and salted almonds, the way the two are so perfect together. Until finally, I'd drive north, allowing you to point out where all the orchards used to grow and all that has changed until we'd park at Charlotte and I'd stop asking questions and we'd sit together without speaking, the skies clearing over the pier, the lake looking a new shade of blue in the light.

A moment of silence, a Quaker moment, in which we listen to the sound of gulls while considering the carousel horses locked in place for the season. A fortifying thing, such silence, so that I might work up the nerve to grab your hand and squeeze it before pointing the car back toward the city and the polling place, where we'd park and enter the booth together, Susan—you who understand better than anyone else how much all of this means.

Come now, and I'll show you the wonder of the machines and the list with all our names. Though I'm greedy when it comes to such pleasures, I am a woman in progress—so come now, sweet Susan, and just this once, I'll let you pull the lever and close the curtain around us.

World without End

THEY CAME TO US from over the lake. Voices transmitted through the buzz of radio, carried through stations that were never quite clear—except during storms or certain times of night, the ionosphere thinning, allowing sound to sweep down from Ontario. Even then, the repetition caused the words to meld into a hum so that the women saying the Rosary sounded like nothing so much as a rush of insects. *As it was in the beginning, is now, and ever shall be.*

The persistent press of prayer was like a spell, like something out of *Rosemary's Baby*. I imagined the Rosary reciters in hooded robes like Mia Farrow's neighbors, crosses gripped to their chests as they kneeled on uncarpeted floor, a circle of grackles forming a sort of rosary of their bent bodies, black beads of supplication.

Sometimes the voices came in French—*Je vous salue, Marie, pleine de grâce*—and not understanding the words and the sound of them, lusher and looser in the mouth, granted the French Rosaries an even greater sense of mystery.

They were with us always, the Rosary ladies.

We might not hear them for a year, but then there they'd be again—in our car as we traveled along the New York State Thruway, inside the broken plaster walls of the house in Albion, following us as we moved onto the reservation near Batavia and into the motel room and apartments that followed, eventually landing with us on the tiny dead-end street in a crowded Rochester neighborhood.

My sisters and brothers might listen a bit before turning the dial in search of music and I must have sneered at the sound, never revealing how drawn I was to the swoop of prayer coming from Erie or Buffalo—even Cleveland, I suppose. For what is the Rust Belt but a bastion of Catholics?

No one I knew ever said them together, the Rosary prayers, excepting mothers, of course, who met in groups in churches or living rooms, carrying strands of beads, some wooden, others crystal or seed pearl. My mother's fervor ebbed and flowed, but when it flowed, it came in scapular-filled waves as she delved into stories of visitations and miracles. The Rosary was pure delight, joint meditation fused onto delicate strands, more rousing than the latest television miniseries or ripest nugget of gossip.

The best rosaries came from cathedrals far away, Paris or Rome. These were practically impossible in my neighborhood but one or two women had them, and how proud they were of their foreign crucifixes and filigreed strings. Others came from the dead, handed down from mothers and great-aunts, the sheen of history absolving the dullness of the beads. Most though were fashioned of glass and came from the shrine near Niagara Falls with an oversized Virgin reigning from atop a giant Plexiglas globe.

But no matter where from or from what material, the women took them up and prayed for relief from bad knees and lost husbands, for better pay, for help with difficult bosses, for the bishop, the pope, and all the saints in heaven. They prayed for upcoming surgeries, full recoveries, for the end of trouble in Northern Ireland, the fall of communism, and thought nothing of following up such lofty intentions with requests for cures for chronic eczema or infected mosquito bites. They prayed for good weather, for weight loss, for help with the electric bill. For difficult children, the resurrection of the dead, for life everlasting and the world without end. Amen.

But the voices on the radio were something other than mothers, something without beginning or end, a channel occasionally opening, an otherworldly hum looming larger than the sounds of home.

Whether the transmission came from a motherhouse in Quebec or a retreat house in Lockport, a single voice called out the first line: *Hail Mary, full of Grace*, followed by the swarm of response: *The Lord is with thee.* The lone voice: *Blessed art though amongst women.* The amalgam of voices: *And blessed is the fruit of thy womb, Jesus.*

The words came and came, the prayers taking on forward motion, barreling over the space between *womb* and *Jesus*, the freight of the line gathering its own speed and rhythm: *thywombjesus*, as if Jesus were the organ and not the fruit, as if He were the one whose womb should be blessed. And what place did meaning have anyway? It was a poetry of sorts, tapping into wells beneath the surface, hitting a place beyond the reach of logic.

It was this that bore down upon me as I listened—whether in English: *Holy Mary, Mother of God*, or French: *Sainte Marie, Mère de Dieu.* The radio voices pushed through the ancient curtain of words, the Hail Marys and the Glory Bes, the prayers not so much the point as the speaking of them together and aloud: *Now and at the hour of our death.* The murmuring a medicine: *And blessed is the fruit of thywombjesus.* Until, at the end of each decade, the women paused for a moment, allowing themselves a collective breath before opening their mouths to begin again.

Mythology

NOW COMES THE SOUND, soft and thumping as a human heart. Who can say whether its source is the teacher as he walks around the classroom tapping the eraser of his pencil against the palm of his hand, or whether the sound comes, as it often does, from the classroom next door?

The teacher one class over has a full-blown crush on the state of Hawaii. He wears shirts covered in hibiscus and returns from school breaks with brown skin and a stack of records he uses to teach the girls in his class how to hula. The sound of drumming slips under the door and into our classroom so that a sway sometimes starts up in my hips. I imagine his girls learning to move their bodies like palm trees in the breeze, and only when I'm safely home do I allow myself to replay the music in my head while turning my hands into birds and watching them take flight.

There's no dancing in our classroom, no red-hot hibiscus, no coconut-scented oil. There is only Mr. Coyle, whose plain dress shirts are topped with ties so short they become stubby arrows pointing to his fleshy midsection, ties that give him the look of a father from a television sitcom—the sort who might have an outburst here or there, but who means well and must rely on his TV wife to set him straight. Rachel Zaso says Mr. Coyle is Italian because his last name ends in a vowel. Rachel wants everyone to be Italian and she's my best friend in the class, so I indulge her—though I wonder why the *e* in *Coyle* doesn't bounce like the vowels in *Travolta* and *Bertinelli* or *Savoia*, the pastry shop a few blocks away from No. 33 School.

Rachel sits in front of me, her ponytail so tight it pulls at the edges of her eyes. Next to her is Tammy Dinkins—and how to account for Tammy, whose father is black and mother is Italian but whose last name ends in *s*? And what of my own last name, which ends in a full-stop *n* and has nothing to do with who I am? Still, I like rules, especially those geared toward the unlocking and understanding of people, so I consider once again what Rachel has said about vowels; is it possible that this is all that remains of sixth grade?

But no, here comes the teacher, his shoes making soft contact with the floor. Arms folded, pencil moving against his hand as he surveys the classroom. He stops from time to time, bending into the flat carpet to remove a scrap of paper or to neaten a pile of books stacked along the wall of windows. Our desks are joined into long rows and we sit, girls and boys contemplating the rectangles of lined paper before us.

When he nears my row and stops tapping, I turn pink and pick up my own pencil, as if I have just that second thought of something to write. The truth is that I've been racking my brain since he gave the assignment and now it's too late. He's in front of me and leaning into my blank page as if checking to see if the words have been written in the very faintest shade of lead.

"How's it going?" His question is gentle but I slink under its weight. I'm the one whose work is normally done while he circulates around the room, offering a thumbs-up or encouraging comments to those who have trouble starting. But now it's as if someone has taken up the classroom globe and spun it hard, leaving me to lurch inside the circle of it, treading the hollow places under the mountain ranges of Central Europe.

The assignment is to write what we want to be someday. One of the most regular questions of childhood, yet it seems I've never been asked it. Maybe because I'm one of seven kids in a family headed by a woman without a husband or a career and we live in a neighborhood brimming with similar women, people who did not plan as children to wait tables or clean hotel rooms or stand around on porches and corners, watching as the world passes. Maybe no one asks because I seem to have it all figured out. I do well in school, where answers to questions about the Thirteen Colonies and the Nile River basin sit like easy treasure inside textbooks. School problems are a universe unto themselves, and I can always be counted on to be the girl with the right answer. But this question stops me. This question whose answer lies in the murky world beyond the classroom.

Besides having children and a job sure to tire her out, one that might eventually give her varicose veins from standing while binding books like my best friend Angie's mother, I've no clue what else a woman might do. I think of Jodi Webber, a girl in my class whose mother drives a pantyhose truck, the way, every morning, Jodi emerges from a van with women's legs painted to its side. I try a quick survey of TV characters for ideas about what women do beyond caring for their families and when nothing comes, I think of my own mother who has worked in factories and shop floors and in the basement of Rochester General Hospital scrubbing down surgical trays. Though she seems grateful for work and tries to make it sound like an adventure, I know she never wanted such jobs, but one thing led to another and there she was, spraying off scalpels and suction devices. I think of the few fathers I know, men with better versions of the same jobs, then consider the most well off families, people who left the neighborhood after landing production jobs at Kodak or Rochester Products—but even with the steady paychecks and annual bonuses allowing them to finance houses in the western suburbs, I understand that these are not the careers we are meant to write.

I look at the back of Rachel Zaso's head, her ponytail moving as she writes, and wish for the first time I could steal another person's answer. If I were in the class next door I'd write *hula dancer* as my career goal and the teacher would stand beside me in his tropical shirt and pat my head with a sun-spotted hand, something blooming in me under such a touch.

But that's next door. In our classroom, Mr. Coyle shifts his weight, the second vowel of his last name waving like a silent flag as he once again begins to strum a pencil against his hand. *Think of what you most enjoy*, he'd advised earlier, but my mind swirls with questions about why some vowels bounce while others don't and how sweet the air surrounding Savoia's on Saturday—then it comes to me. What I most enjoy is checking out books from the Sully Branch Library, taking them home and reading them under a tent made of my blanket and knees. I'm partial to mysteries and travel books but can't get enough Greek mythology. The thrill of Athena bursting out of her father's head, the fully clothed answer to a headache. The story of the nymph so in love with Apollo she sits staring into the sun until the gods take pity and turn her into a sunflower. Arachne, the over-proud weaver, comparing herself to the gods. I like nothing better than to sit inside my blue blanket tent taking in stories of golden apples and pomegranates and unexpected transformations. So far removed from anything I know, but familiar too, the unpredictability of the gods and the longing of mortals. And just like that, I make up my mind about my career: *mythologist*.

I've never heard of the job before, but I remember what Mr. Coyle said—*You can do anything; don't limit yourselves*—and write it down. It looks good on the page, the way it ends in *-ologist*, like something a person might need to go to college to study. I check the spelling and prepare myself for the shine in Mr. Coyle's face, the one that comes when he takes my paper and holds it up as an example to the rest of the class, the pain of so many eyes on me mingled with the thrill of having my work publicly praised. When I'm finally prepared for the terrible and wondrous flare of attention, I look up. Only instead of shine, there's something new in Mr. Coyle's face.

His eyes are a thick squint. He's removed his glasses and rubs his lids, as if the entire state of Hawaii with all its sun has come into the room and blinded him temporarily. He tilts his head then straightens himself with a jerk, the way people do when falling in dreams. Mr. Coyle does not touch my paper, does not lift it to the class, saying, "Listen to this, boys and girls." He only returns his glasses to his face and says, *Well, now, that's a new one.* He smiles, but the way he says it, his surprise—*Well, now*—tells me that mythology is no kind of career. People must find something better with which to occupy their time than stories of girls who slip into the undersides of meadows while gathering poppies and don't know enough to keep from eating sugared-up pomegranate seeds.

I listen as other kids take turns reading their answers, voices trumpeting intentions to be fashion models, astronauts, the next Michael Jackson. Their goals sound impossible, but must be correct because they include no job anyone I know has ever done.

You can do anything.

Mr. Coyle does not teach us to hula nor wear shirts teeming with exotic flowers, but drives a bright green Volkswagen bug and even beeps at us sometimes. He's strict—too strict, some say—but while I enjoy all the reading he assigns and the occasional games of Heads-Up, Seven-Up, it's the easy order of his class that lets me love my time there.

But saying we can do anything? It seems too large to be true, too wide to pin down. I cover the word *mythologist* with a hand and listen to other kids read their goals, trying my best to think of another career—something beyond the study of hula music, long-gone goddesses, and the tender cycling of the world.

Capias

HERE SHE COMES NOW, *la novia*, the bride, and how everyone turns to stare.

My God, *mira su traje*, look at the sight of her gown, and *que hermosa*, how lovely, as she points a satin shoe in our direction and steps into view, this bride from thirty years gone by. She'll have children by now, our bride, grandchildren perhaps. But not yet. Not in this moment, where she stands before the altar, a line of saints watching from beneath the panel of stained glass. Her back is to us, pearls running down the length of her gown, train puddled at her feet, the runner like snow upon the aisle, girls in chiffon dresses at her side.

She's skinny, this bride, her bronzed clavicles making knives just under the lace—but this is a wedding and everything swells with the day so that her body ripens as she stands before us. She was always pretty with her pocketful of sharp features, but on this day light shows in her face as she walks down the center aisle of Corpus Christi and stands before the padre, whose Spanish has never been perfected but whose kindness burns in his wide Irish face. And *ay Dios mío*, look at the groom—compact and good-looking, tux and new shoes, the whole of him decked out in white, the way men used to do—the way he nearly bursts with pride as she reaches his side, then as he fades away, becoming nothing so much as the spray of baby's breath in his pocket until only she remains. It's the bride we look for anyway. When wedding parties emerge from the churches— the flash of white—*there she is*, we say, something starting in us.

The bride, I say, *oh look!* I've seen her beside the pink chapel in midtown Memphis, under the lilacs at Highland Park and gathering jasmine in the garden of the Alcázar in Sevilla. The bride. An ordinary woman making silk of just one day—the beginning, like all beginnings, belonging to more than just herself.

But back to our bride, *la novia tan hermosa*, and the way she lets go of her flowers in the church hall after Mass. The way she dances with her new groom—a slow song, something rising between them, burning beneath the satin, but not so much that she can't stand to dance with her father and the line of other men who slip folded bills into the purse tied to her waist. It's 1980 in western New York; there's nothing shameful about a dollar dance. All we see is how well she dances, the way she becomes a sweep of lace with every turn, each man taken in for a few seconds then spun away as the next arrives.

Now she's dancing with someone from the band, the conga player, or the singer who holds the *güiro* in one hand, the metal *púa* in the other, making the sounds that the body knows better than words. Everyone joins the dance. Children wiggle narrow hips between chugs of cold *maltas* and sips of piña coladas. These are Puerto Rican families, salsas and merengues are as natural as bottles of rum and the bride's basket of *capias*—wedding favors made by her mother and her sisters, charms surrounded by bits of satin and tulle, miniature corsages bearing the couples' names and wedding date.

Our bride takes a break and carries her *capias* in a basket, pinning one to each female guest, bending into ladies too old to rise, *viejas*, kissing them once on the cheek, *Bendición*, asking for a blessing and giving another kiss at their reply, *Que Dios te bendiga, mi niña* (May God bless you, my child).

She moves on, the number of *capias* dwindling as she approaches—but what's this, a white child at her wedding? Other than the priest who's already returned to the rectory, the girl is the only *blanca* in the crowd. Oh yes, she recognizes her now, the one always with the Rosas girls—Wandi and Sari and Maritza. We both wonder whether she should pin one to me, this girl who has somehow landed at her reception, but here it comes, a bit of lace stuck to my dress, just enough to comprehend some of what it means to be a bride, the lightness and grace, the moment suspended, a respite from the daily business of living, if only for a few hours. *La novia*, not so much a person as a condition, wrapped in white and handing out favors. What does she say as she pins it? I'm not old enough to be asked to give a blessing, not fluent enough to ask to receive one. She probably says *thank you for coming*, and maybe I know enough to mumble *congratulations* as I touch the bit of plumage from her basket.

We stand together, a strange child at a wedding and a bride with her basket of *capias*. How fast it will go, thirty years. The gown gone ivory, the rasp of *güiro* fading into the hum of tree frogs. But not yet.

Let us stay a little longer in the basement of Corpus Christi Church, for the beer and the *pasteles*, and the sound of the band starting up. This time it's an old song and the *viejas* sigh while I let my fingers leave the *capia* pinned to my dress and run to find my friends and beg a share of cake. The day is still before us, and *ay, Dios mío*, what a beautiful bride, and yes, *que todos estamos bendecidos*—we are, each of us, in this moment, blessed.

The Last American Virgin

IN MY MEMORY, THE virgin is French. Halo of dark curls, mouth the color of pomegranate, as if those from an Old World fresco. Or maybe she only seemed French because of the way, in those days, the word itself was salacious—something to do with the body, a special kind of kissing, *frenching*, people called it. The word belonged to me more than my sisters. We each had different fathers and mine's last name was DesJardin; his Frenchness was one of the few details my mother revealed—that, and his two-timing—so that the concept of *French* was further tainted by its connection to him. Later, I'd learn to like the language that sounded like a mouth swollen with delicious things, but back then, *French* was a way to talk dirty, like the time my mother got a whiff of the perfume I'd spritzed on my pink velour blouse while at Angie VanEpps's house. "My God," she said. "You smell like a French whore."

But back to the virgin. It turns out that I was wrong about her being French. I'd run two films together: Diane Franklin, the actress from the 1982 film *The Last American Virgin*, played a French exchange student in another teen romance a few years later. The two roles collided inside my head, so that she was also French as the virgin, all dewy eyes and red cushion mouth as she arrives at her new school and becomes the target of the bad boy—the one who will use her and toss her aside, the one she cannot help but fall for, surrendering her virginity and becoming pregnant in one fell swoop. Of course, she's ditched. But all is not lost. There's another boy waiting in the wings, one who's loved her from afar, one who sells his stereo equipment to pay for the procedure, the one who brings her to the clinic, presenting her with a bag of oranges after the abortion—so that to me, in 1982, the giving of oranges became the most generous expression of love.

A body becomes what it holds. When it carries a baby the body becomes a mother. When it clings to desire the body makes itself into a tooth. My body carried what it learned in middle school classes—the proper use of prepositions, the Three-Fifths Compromise, a series of facts about internal organs. *The heart is the size of a clenched fist; situated between the lungs, it pumps thousands of gallons of blood per day.* In 1982 I was a color-coded diagram of left and right ventricles and inferior vena cava.

Even our school was named for the body: Corpus Christi—Body of Christ in Latin. Our colors were white and red, for the body and the blood. Though the school shared a parking lot with the church of the same name, the parish no longer supported the school, and except for the few of us who crossed the parking lot for Holy Day Masses, the school seemed Catholic in name only. Situated between neighborhoods where poverty and teen pregnancy loomed larger than any catechism, crucifixes may have been affixed to walls or a cracked plaster Virgin pushed into the corner of a classroom, but kids came to Corpus regardless of religious background or parish affiliation. Theology class shared time with sex education, so that we learned about the workings of the fallopian tubes after studying the beatitudes. *Blessed are the poor in heart: for they will see God*, followed by *the epithelium is covered with cilia that beat continuously toward the uterus.*

Catholic school, but more like an outreach program to inner-city kids run by the Sisters of St. Joseph. No bottled sexuality, no shaming of students who chased each other during lunch break, boys corralling girls into the back of the parking lot where the fence was broken and the hedge grew wild.

"Stop that," a teacher or lunch mother might call out, and "Leave those girls alone." But the Sisters in their Birkenstocks and plain skirts seemed at home in their bodies, and even when religion reared its head, nothing was trumpeted so much as love.

The body is what it carries, and since the Sisters said we were children of God, surely we carried goodness, which meant the body itself was good. Even if they'd tried to send different messages, who could have been fooled about the pleasures of the body? Why else would the boys run so hard, arms flailing, reaching out in the shadows of the back lot while we crossed our arms over newly budded breasts, protecting ourselves from the very same force they celebrated. Why else would we—so skilled in the shooing away of the boys—sometimes let ourselves be touched?

Even as a Catholic girl, I was first and foremost a poor girl, and my virginity was not so much a virtue as salvation. Any fear I had about letting myself be swept up was less about purity than the ability to transform my body into another kind of vessel. A vessel to carry poetry by Langston Hughes alongside facts about the human heart and strings of perfectly diagrammed sentences. A vessel to transport me from an inner-city parking lot. My body was an airship then, leaning into wing and wind, and I strove only to leave room enough to someday have a chance at flight.

It's easy to see why I mixed them up, those 1980s movies. Neither was high art. They were only two of many teen movies featuring pods of boys trying to get lucky. Films in which beautiful girls were inevitably duped by bad boys, who cocked and strutted and got what they wanted but who eventually fell from grace, thereby allowing the goodhearted misfit to emerge as victor and claim the girl, who always served as the prize. Whether the movies were set in high schools or summer camps, the lessons were the same: (1) girls often made bad choices where boys where concerned; (2) lovers could go from sweet-talking to heartless in the space of an hour; but (3) goodness always won out in the end.

Besides the sight of a boy bringing oranges to the girl he loves, the reason *The Last American Virgin* stands out—even after all these years—is because it was the only movie of its sort to veer from the formula, the one film in which love and kindness do not prevail.

By middle school I'd learned the fruitlessness of being a good girl. I no longer cared to be the highest scorer on the weekly spelling test. It was no longer enough to know the answer before everyone else. Most of all, I wanted Sister Eileen to swoop into my classroom with a small wrapped box that might contain a bracelet or necklace or even a rosary, I suppose—for nothing speaks of possibility like a small wrapped box.

Sister Eileen was the principal, a woman with short dark hair and an easy smile who reminded me of Shirley Feeney from *Laverne & Shirley*. I wanted her to walk over to my desk with a wrapped box like she'd done with Louise Baird, whose blonde hair and sweet features belied a badness so spectacular that even the Puerto Rican girls were impressed.

The gift Sister Eileen gave Louise was a small flip-up alarm clock meant to remedy her habit of tardy arrivals. It might have been a cast-off, from a garage sale, the sort of thing no one would ever want. But the gentleness with which it was delivered and the way the Sisters of St. Joseph version of Shirley Feeney waited with such expectation made it clear that even our principal was head over heels for the baddest girl at school.

"There," I said to myself while watching Louise unwrap the tiny package under the watch of the entire class, everyone leaning in as she took her time with the tape. "Here's what I want."

Virginity never made sense as commodity, as if an action of the body (verb) was something to be given away (noun), an object to be taken or stolen, as if it were a gold coin. The loss of it was especially hard to fathom, for it seemed to me not even a discrete event. In theory it was clear enough: a girl succumbed, let a boy into her body, and there it went—her virginity evaporated like water in the desert. But the world seemed murkier than that, the actions we took sloppier and by degree—so many ways of touching, so many ways to open oneself to another.

Of course, I understood the technical rules for avoiding sex and must have bought in on some level, understanding the precise actions to be avoided and letting myself go only so far, sneering at loose girls and feeling strong at my refusals, but even then, my actions were based more on fear than goodness. And even if I sometimes managed goodness, where was the reward in that? Halos were for the holy, a virtue that extended beyond mere goodness. Holiness demanded more than sensible decisions; it required not only the forgoing of pleasure, for instance, but also the seeking out and endurance of suffering. Beatrice of Nazareth was said to have worn a girdle of thorns. Catherine of Siena refused food. Such women were admired by the world, their lives celebrated, their images kept alive on prayer cards, where they were rendered with sweet sad smiles, and outfitted with roses and halos.

Saints aren't the only ones given halos. Jesus gets one, of course, as does Our Lady, who is often depicted with light crowning her head—she may be the mortal most likely to be haloed, in fact, so much do we adore the Virgin. In early frescos, the Madonna is topped by yellow discs of light. The Byzantines added gold leaf, encircling the Virgin's head with thick helmets of gold. Renaissance masters were more delicate: Raphael's halos are thin ribbons, Botticelli's are barely visible, while Sassoferrato's are more like radiant fuzz. Later artists chose halos dependent upon mood or scene (or patrons' preferences), sometimes depicting Our Lady with intricately gilded crowns or translucent mantles, while at other times adorning her with garlands of roses or ciclets of hovering stars.

Where were the halos for girls who did not let the boys touch them for too long under their butter yellow uniform shirts, who resisted the warm slip of hand in the shadows of the school? Girls who helped their mothers with dishes without complaint, who remembered to say *please* and *thank you* and tried hard not to let themselves get hickeys on the weekend of their confirmations? Such girls were neither venerated nor lavished with light. Whether the decision to stay virgins was made as a gift to our eventual husbands (as it had been for our mothers) or to provide us with a shot at better lives—we made it. And if life imitated art and everyday goodness was rewarded with gold leaf spangles blooming from my head every time I did my homework or said *no*, well, then virtue might have been enough.

And so I learned to be bad enough to be sent to Sister Eileen's office while remaining good enough to hedge my bets in case there might be something more in store for me. There were no counselors in Catholic schools, at least not in poorly funded inner-city schools like Corpus Christi, but Sister Eileen was a good listener, and no matter what nonsense came from my mouth, she'd laugh and shake her head.

"What happened next?" she'd say while moving about her office with her work, or "Why do you think that?"

I'd never seen everyday nuns depicted in paintings or tapestries, and if they were, they certainly were not given halos. I thought of the priests and bishops, their words and actions highlighted and praised by the Church while the legion of Sisters facing the children of a dying city day after day were as invisible as the girls they taught to write their names in cursive, as instructed, on the upper-left side of their papers. *Who made the rules about boys and girls anyway?* I wondered. *And why should women be vessels of goodness, when some of its very best practitioners went unnoticed by the world?*

Humility is a decent enough virtue. But there were times when the covering of the body while the boys ran hard and shouted their desire seemed a burden by comparison. Because when it comes down to it—no matter how shy or how good or how kind—what person does not want to fling herself into the face of the world and be properly regarded (seen and heard and maybe even admired) if only just once in her life?

Her timing was perfect. Named for her mother who was in turn named for Our Lady, Madonna's *Like a Virgin* album came out in 1984 and nothing was ever the same. The singer offended and enthralled, using the word *virgin* to call up images of the Holy Mother, pairing baubles and bustiers with sacred symbols and baring herself to the world—this woman named for the mother of God whose every last cell simmered sex.

On the album cover, Madonna sprawls onto satin sheets, body pushing out of white lace that stands no chance of containing it. Flowers in her lap and wearing a pearl choker, she's a sultry bride. Smoky eyes, mouth partly opened, as if captured between expectant breaths. No gilded crown sits atop her tousled hair, no light emanates from her body, but allure surrounds her like a nimbus, so that Madonna becomes, in 1984, the virgin most worthy of veneration.

I'd transferred from the all-girl Nazareth Academy to the local public high school, trading in uniforms for tight jeans and torn sweatshirts inspired by Jennifer Beals in *Flashdance*. Nineteen eighty-four, a time of coming undone. I attended Mass of my own accord—drinking in the language and the symbols, the incense, the altar cloth—and was ripe for the mixing of the thump of desire with the icons of the Church.

My friends were similarly struck. We strung our wrists with black bangles, practiced penciling beauty marks above puckered snarls, sewed skirts that fitted like slinky tubes over our legs, imagined the cool weight of the belt she wore, the words *Boy Toy* falling beneath an exposed belly. We all wore lace dresses to prom, donned long gloves and cut our hair into wavy bobs, remaking ourselves as best we could into the woman on the album cover. We wanted the boldness—the way she behaved more like a boy than any girl we ever knew—but the lined eyes and lace dress were easier to duplicate.

My favorite Virgin was the statue at church. She was serene, standing up on the altar day after day, candles flickering at her feet, surrounded by all those statues of serious men with their pens and chiseled faces— there she was, presiding calmly in front of the church, her robe the color of morning glories.

In the early years, Our Lady was strung with a garland of plastic roses that some part of me knew was tacky, even as a kid from a house with paneling and mismatched chairs. But the flowers also made her seem worldly somehow, as if she made trips to Hawaii or Aruba after everyone slipped from the church—I imagined the Virgin hovering up and over the roof with a suitcase and her garland of flowers. Still I did not miss them once they were gone, the pink flowers—only the idea of them, which is a different thing entirely.

The body is built for many things. Hauling and walking, studying and pleasure, creating and healing. Mine might have been built for a boy, but I waited and instead gave it to a man, so that body became just right for a motel room and the sound of a voice giving directions I didn't understand, in part because I was frozen, but also because the words became lush in his Cuban mouth. *Cloz yu ice*, took minutes to unravel. *Close your eyes.* It's no less than miraculous the way the body adapts, so that I found that I was built for closing my eyes, for the tube top I wore, the green bedspread, and the taste of beer in the mouth of another.

The body persists. One day it will be older than seventeen and better understand the many ways of loving and giving and coming undone. But first I am seventeen in a rented bed, the technical requirements for the loss of virginity met, though I feel no loss, nothing changing in me except the memorizing of the pattern of a strange ceiling and realizing that in this as in many other things, more fuss had been made than was warranted. What looms larger than the mechanics of that day or the memory of the bedspread is the betrayal that follows. He has another woman, I learn. The man with the green eyes and mash of lush words has lied. When I understand this, then and only then, do I feel the loss of something like a gold coin.

Which brings me to the end of *The Last American Virgin*, where the good boy has sold everything to pay for his beloved's abortion. The beautiful girl finally kisses him and it's like birds soaring, the feeling of seeing our sweet boy finally rewarded. She invites him to her eighteenth birthday party the next week; he arrives with a locket, only to find her back in the arms of the one who'd used her in the first place. Everything stops in the moment of her looking over her shoulder at the good boy, the one she will never love. And the boy, the one who'd loved so openly, has no choice but to turn and leave, locket clenched in hand, tears streaking his face.

I think of the end of the 1980s film and begin to understand that virginity is not about refusal, the saying of *no* a thousand and one times, nor the granting of halos and crowns.

The body becomes what it gives up too, I suppose, so that the loss of virginity is marked by the movement of the human heart from chart and diagram to muscle and smooth pink flesh. It is the gathering up of left and right ventricle, the stashing of inferior and superior vena cava into a bag like oranges, and the bringing of them to a misguided French girl who looks over her shoulder but does not see the treasure of what is offered. It is saying *yes* to another despite the hard stone the world sometimes shows itself to be. The loss of virginity is all of this and more. It is the opening of the rind with one's fingers. It is the revelation of the tenderest flesh, the lifting of it and placing it into the waiting mouth of another.

Peace

I

IT'S POSSIBLE THOSE TIMES on the side of the road were not as peaceful as I recall. Hair might have stuck in clumps to sweaty necks, gnats may have swarmed, tensions might have run high. But I remember grass tall enough to tickle the backs of knees, a breeze making flutter of maple leaves, the clop of an Amish buggy as it passed. The guards on the other side of the fence—boys really— stood in uniformed lines, quiet except for the fact of their weapons and what they might need to do should one of our group disobey the law and scale the fence between us and them. Climbing the fence was a real possibility, one of the reasons for our drive to the region. Carved by the glacial scrape of the Laurentide Ice Sheet, the Finger Lakes became a land of water and sky, where the Iroquois lived before the encroachment of the British and French—and us, in our cars and vans traveling to the Seneca Army Depot, which was said to house the largest stockpile of nuclear weapons in the country.

Nineteen eighty-three. The Cold War wasn't over, and talk of nuclear weapons and Soviets was part of daily life. Thousands of activists descended on the depot in the summer, setting up a Women's Peace Encampment in an old farmhouse nearby. They came in buses and airplanes and sometimes on foot from all over the States to protest. The women nailed peace signs to trees, painted flowers and doves onto the sides of barns, scrawled slogans against nukes and the men who made them. Hundreds were arrested; women from the encampment and others who'd flocked to the area, including groups from Buffalo, Rochester, and Syracuse, progressives who packed into vans, staring into cornfields and vineyards and the blue of lakes as we passed, eventually unloading outside the gates of the depot, where we stood holding hands and singing peace songs.

I'm not sure I fully understood the threat of nuclear weapons. I knew what weapons were, of course, and must have understood at least some of why we were there, but nothing made as much sense as the strip of land between road and depot, the way it was dotted with goldenrod and chicory. Someone set an embroidered runner and vase of wildflowers onto a small table in a mowed section of grass, transforming it into an altar, the patch of weeds into a church. With the folk choir and the gleam of golden guitars, those masses for peace were like field trips to me. I should feel shame at admitting such a thing, given how old I was (ninth grade), what was at stake (nuclear armament), and the fact that the masses usually ended with someone climbing the fence and falling over. But even then, the bodies hoisted over the coil of barbed wire were received so gently by the open hands of the military boys, their landings cushioned by the grass nuzzling the fence's interior, so that, in memory, the protests became a sort of ballet, the call of crows joined by the folk group singing Cat Stevens's songs, everything on both sides of the fence framed by the sway of maple trees.

II

How can I say I was a soldier for peace when I worried so much about how my hair would come out in my mug shot? I wore it long and curly then and wondered if the waves had held during so many hours of sitting-in. I'd allowed a smile to ruin the perfect scowl of my face when one of the arresting officers flirted while fastening my arms, setting me in the paddy wagon with such care, we might have been on a date.

Nineteen ninety-one. Invasion in the Gulf. U.S. Forces sent to fight in Iraq, thousands dead. Eight years after the depot masses, I was old enough to understand, old enough to care, and decided it was time to scale my own fences instead of staring into drifts of pretty weeds. The protest itself came after weeks of planning and discussing tactics—peaceful resistance and how to make your body go limp while resisting arrest. Finally, we made our way as a group to the federal building in downtown Rochester, the twelve of us calling ourselves the *D'Amato Dozen* after the conservative state senator we'd targeted. Our coup was convincing his secretary to buzz us into the tiny office. She'd had her suspicions, D'Amato's secretary, but eleven of us slipped behind a partition while the most confident sweettalked: "We have a package to deliver," he said. "Please open the door."

She saw what it might mean and wrung her hands and said she wasn't sure; but he was persuasive—"Just a crack," he said—his voice so velvet that our lady of the hidden buzzer could not hold out. One crack was all it took for a foot, an arm—and before you knew it, all twelve of us had stormed inside. And yes, it was lying, but somehow okay because we were for peace after all.

Our sit-in was followed by arrest—a successful action, all things considered. But how to square it with the memory of the secretary who did not relax the entire time we occupied the office, never once settling into her seat, and even when we sang never once looking at us with anything but fear? No matter how sweet our "Kumbaya"s, how heartfelt our "If I Had a Hammer"s, no matter how gilded our hunger or how exquisite our patience, she never stopped twisting those hands.

Our intentions were good—there was real invasion in the Gulf, after all, thousands of lives lost, governments gone wrong, families gunned down in the street. What is one person's discomfort or a well-intentioned lie in the face of such realities?

I can only say that when I look back on those hours, the paddy wagon and the fingerprinting, the handsome officer with his smile and the subsequent court dates, I remember most of all the secretary shaking her head as she wept, looking at us and saying, "I'm sorry I ever trusted you."

III

The rectories of Roman Catholic churches are ordinarily reserved for priests, but there was nothing ordinary about our parish. In the more robust days, several priests shared the rectory, but by the 1970s Corpus Christi had only one priest. By the late 1980s the progressive priest decided to leave the rectory for a home a few miles from the church and offered the rectory to college students who made peanut butter sandwiches for the homeless and filled out Mass cards in exchange for rent.

There were four of us: the oldest, a graduate student (who collected Victrolas and taught me to make ricotta pie), two Eastman School students (earnest blonds from the Midwest, the sounds of piano and cello leaking from their rooms), and me. We lived together, all of us posting flyers announcing visiting liberation theologians, taking turns ushering people in for nonviolence study groups, making nightly rounds to lock the huge old building, keeping the hub of the large urban church occupied so our priest could live in a grittier section of the city, closer to the neighborhood from which I'd only recently escaped and nearer those he hoped to serve—though I sometimes wondered if he simply required respite from the nonstop trinity of midnight callers (the mentally ill, inebriated, and confessional).

I'd been baptized at Corpus Christi as a baby, had slept inside a roll of carpet as a child, finding the opening after running way from my mother during Easter Vigil Mass, refusing to come out of hiding, frozen as the statues taken down from the altar on Good Friday, all of them crowding the side sacristy, all dark shadows and cracked plaster showing in moonlight. I'd come to Mass willingly and often on my own—looking forward to the homilies, the way they helped make sense of the world, the words washing over me, the names of faraway places, sounding like poems read at school. So while it may have surprised my friends when I applied for the opening to live in the rectory community, it made perfect sense to me. Corpus Christi had always been home.

And so I lived in the rectory with a handful of others, reading Thomas Merton and Desmond Tutu, sitting around a candle in the evenings, considering peace from all its flickering angles. So much feeling welling up, so much talk of social justice. Cesar Chavez and the grape boycott and fasting three days for El Salvador and breaking the fast with cheap wine, the highs and the lows. Talk of twelve steps and self-help and the reading of books with rainbows flanking their covers. Marches on Washington and white cotton sundresses and men drawn to such dresses like flies. A time of Advent and Lent and clear Octobers and cider—and our German visitor teaching me to say pumpkin in German (*kürbis*), how handsome he was and how new I felt and his chest the color of oak leaves, the Berlin Wall coming down while he visited, the sound of his voice breaking in the kitchen while talking with a sister he hadn't heard in years. The volume of Yevtushenko found in an old bookcase.

But for all the poetry, for all the study groups and talk of hopes and fears deep into the night, the echo of piano and cello, for all the rallies and demonstrations for peace—the truth is that I lived in the rectory for other reasons. Despite the fact that formal prayer often felt like a pile of pebbles set onto my tongue, in truth, I loved the old building and its many rooms precisely because it was a church.

Some mornings I'd slip out into the church before anyone else woke and sit facing the sanctuary. To some, the oversized nave with its rows of old pews and high ceilings might have seemed hollow or cold. But the old wood warmed me, the ceiling beams felt like a backbone and the statues of the saints—the same sets of bony features that frightened me as I made the rounds to lock up the old building at night—softened as morning came, their faces taking on the sheen of familiarity, becoming old friends in the early light.

I'd sit for a while, experiencing a sort of quiet joy I'd never found at rallies and lectures and study groups. Everything fell away. Worries about past and future, thoughts of what to do next. There was only the sound of birds on Prince Street, the scent of balsam and cleaning wax, the great panel of stained glass breaking into a wash of blues and greens, and all the candles along the altar waiting to be lit.

Our Lady of the Carpeted Stairs

I'M NOT THE ONE who placed the Virgin outside the priest's office.
But when he stood by my side and said *I'm onto you* with a wink,
I went along with it. I'd long ago acquired the habit of hiding how
little I knew and more than that, I feared losing that speck of connection, the small but meaningful space between the Father's wink
and his words: *I'm onto you.*

I had no father of my own, just the story of a man who'd traveled the New York State Thruway selling vacuum cleaners, stopping
between Albany and Buffalo for a bite to eat, a soft reception. We'd
only been an off-ramp to him, my mother and I, which may explain
why I'd been trying to connect with the one called *Father* since I was
a child. And because I had no arsenal of obvious charms at my disposal, I used what I knew to lure him, whipping up storms in the gulf
of my mouth and sending them his way, twisted ribbons of longing.

I was twenty when the wink arose between us but remembered
when, years before, he was new to the parish, a fresh-scrubbed priest
walking our neighborhood, shining his light on streets others refused
to enter. He most loved a girl whose last name was a stew of delicious
syllables—LaMarata—a name that sounded to me like a prayer. She
was sick and the Father kept a picture that LaMarata had colored
hanging beside his rectory desk. He must have looked at it every
day, taking in the crayoned lines on his way in and out of the office,
staring into the mash of flowers, making a point of remembering the
dying child, the brevity of life, the way nothing is guaranteed. And

how low I was that I envied the girl the purity of her illness, when all those years before, a good priest appeared suddenly among us, back when I was nothing so much as a little hurricane, before the wink and the words *I'm onto you.*

When the wink came, I was living in the rectory and there were times—certain mornings, or the hour between Sunday Masses—when the door to his office flung wide and the priest tumbled forth as if propelled by a gust of wind, spilling toward the piano in the living room. I'd hear the start of the keys and slip down the stairs, sitting on a step just out of sight and listening to what came from his playing, something hard and loose and far from the precision of the piano student from Missouri. For all this talk, it might seem as if I loved the priest the way some girls take to older men, the way some parishioners fall for ministers. But no, he was simply a man whose goodness intrigued me. First, that such goodness could exist, and second, that it was directed so firmly at the world apart from me.

Is my delight so hard to imagine then—the warmth of the wink, the familiarity of the words? *I'm onto you.* The only real surprise was the speed with which I offered up my gummy smile, the ease with which I neither confirmed nor denied, and in my silence pretended I had indeed placed the statue of the Blessed Mother outside his office door.

And when, the next morning, the Virgin appeared on the landing of the stairs near my room, I stood open-mouthed like Bernadette in her cave at Massabielle or Lúcia dos Santos dropping the bundle of sticks she'd collected when the Lady showed herself at Fátima. I became faithful pilgrim and startled peasant girl as I stood there, the sight of Our Lady of the Carpeted Stairs nearly causing me to fall backward.

Then I remembered—*I'm onto you*—and though I had not started this game, I laughed and laid claim, hauling the waist-high statue into my room. She became a shared joke then, the Virgin, going back and forth between us: under a kitchen table, in the little-used office on the third floor, behind the drapery in the large meeting room. More smiles and winks, Our Lady becoming a sort of holy baton, an invisible string connecting the two of us—winks and more winks—until the night I placed her on the lid of the closed toilet in the priest's private bathroom.

I'd walked into his office a few times before, enjoying the view through his window, the small patch of grass, the line of books, staring at the coloring made by the sick child all those years before. I wandered in again the night I placed the Virgin on the toilet lid, taking a seat and staring at the same water stain in the ceiling that had been there since I was a girl. All the times I'd been in that office as a child: dragged in by my mother for the humiliation of family counseling, for my firing as an altar girl ten years prior, stopping by to say hello before Thursday night folk Masses, shifting my feet while making up questions in an attempt to hold him. The same office I'd occupy a few years later, sitting beside the man I'd marry, his voice ratcheting with each word spoken, nervousness translating into volume because he was modest and a Lutheran and what had he ever done to deserve interrogation about heaven, the saints, and accepting children with open arms should they come?

But that was future and past, and as I sat in the priest's office on that night, hands resting on the head of the Virgin, I only stared out the window trying to decide the next move in a game I'd lacked the boldness to invent.

How did it come to me then, the bathroom?

It wasn't that I didn't revere Our Lady. I'd always admired Mary, not praying to her so much as finding comfort in her presence. As a child, I'd listened to the stories of our religion—the water and the wine, Mary and Gabriel, Lazarus's return from the dead—and seen them as a dream blossoming just under the surface of the everyday world, a beautiful dream, one shared and dipped into during Mass. But one day something tipped me off, a thing said at church, someone hinting at the reality of Mary made pregnant without sex, so that I had no choice but to quiz anyone who'd answer, asking about the matter over and over: *Do you really believe?* I persisted beyond politeness, thinking people too shy to speak, thinking they'd lumped Mary in with Santa Claus, magical stories they safeguarded for children. I asked until their faces turned, eyebrows rising, foreheads gathering into lines—until I finally understood. Others believed differently. Literally. I was perhaps alone in the dream. I continued coming to Mass but backed off from saying things I didn't believe. But not from Mary, never from Mary—the lone figure of a woman among men, the one soft spot you could count on in any church—and because a woman becoming pregnant without a husband was what I knew best, I required no magic to adore her.

Even as I lifted the statue and placed the Virgin in the bathroom, I never thought to offend. I wanted only to succeed in this game and required a place that had not yet been tried, and there it was. A tiled grotto complete with raised platform. And when, the next morning, the priest did not smile or wink, when he did not even look in my direction and the air between us became as thick as it ever had been, and Our Lady failing to appear to me again, I knew I'd taken things too far—which, in reality, was less disappointment than confirmation, for I have always had a way of taking things too far.

I'm onto you.

I suppose that more than anything I feared that the priest had always been onto me in some meaningful way—as if with his goodness he was able to spot its opposite in the blustery child and ten years later, in the wide-eyed woman living in his former rooms. I was nothing like the girl with the illness, the one whose name would always be the sound of a prayer. I was nothing like the statue of Our Lady, sweet and pink and waiting to be moved—I asked too many questions, was a tad too fast with the wisecrack, and there was a hunger about me that fell in strange shapes from my eyes. How much more difficult, adoration, in the living breathing world.

Twenty years have come and gone, and still how little I know. Except that he was wrong about the Virgin. I was not the one who lifted her by the slender waist and set her blue and blooming before his door.

I was simply the one who stared into the faded colors of another girl's picture, trying to unravel the mechanics of adoration from the way she crayoned her lines. The one crouched on the staircase on certain Sundays, listening to the mess of music rise from the piano, the sound as choppy and glorious as a springtime storm. The one whose heart pounded as the sound came, caught up in something I could not name as he played. The one who sat watching the Father as he rose from the bench, headed back to his office, letting the door close all the way behind him.

II

Do you remember
The night we were lost
In the shade of the blackthorn
And the touch of the frost?

ANONYMOUS, seventeenth-century Irish

A Party, in May

HOW DOES ONE NIGHT set itself apart from all the others?
So many nights, even in half a lifetime. Nights of twinkling lights
and wedding tents and the moon hanging like a Chinese lantern.
Nights of almond oil and the catalpa with its heart-shaped leaves,
nights when the body has no choice but to unburden itself and the
wreck of sheets at the end of the bed. Nights of the box fan churning
heat in an August room, the movement of blades, a touch of hand
shivering the skin. Nights without enough hours to pour the words
into, and if it's winter, nights of brandy and pine boughs thrown into
the fire—needles becoming fireworks, how they crackle, what scent
they give. But there are other nights too. Nights of tight words and
forced music, nights of the candle dying out and the chill that won't
leave, nights of slammed doors and falling into bed alone, hands over
your eyes. Nights of staring into the ceiling, looking for signs in the
woodwork. Nights of tossing and turning and trying to remember
that morning will come. In all those thousands of nights, why should
this be the one?

The snow, I suppose—though snow itself is not rare in New York
State. But this snow was different. Nothing like the snow of holiday
greeting cards—this snow inserted itself into the wrong season and
made demands, threatening the redbuds and the lilacs. And it was not
just any night. We were well into the month of May, the evening before
Mother's Day—the night of a party, a party that would have been

unlikely in December, and impossible in the month of April. Some nights must happen exactly as they do and this one was set for May.

We'd gathered to celebrate three birthdays—a good friend, a sister, and my husband. All turning thirty. We used the hall at the apartment complex where we lived, a fine complex; the wide room was newly carpeted and flanked by a dance floor and a granite-topped bar with a view to a pool not yet open for the season. A newly planted magnolia tree stood sentry near the door, a ring of fresh mulch circling its base, its fuzzy pods opening to flowers that showed pink. The magnolia's blossoms sprouting from bare branches were what I first thought of when the snow came.

It was not the best of parties, nor was it a particularly beautiful May. It is simply a place to begin. As in any story, the roots extend beyond the beginning, going back to a time before the month was called May, before birthday cakes, before invitations stuffed into envelopes and sent. Like the olive trees of Lebanon are most stories, thousands of years' worth of roots fingering the undersides of things. *The Sisters Olive Trees of Noah*, the Lebanese trees are called, because they're said to have been the source of the branch the dove brought back to Noah, a branch signifying the waning of floodwaters, the end of God's wrath. The trees still stand there in Lebanon, sixteen of them spreading their gnarled branches over the village of Bechealeh, going on with the business of bearing fruit as they have done since the time the land was called Canaan. Which brings me to the Hebrew Scriptures, to Abraham, and to Sarah.

I'd devoured the illustrated Children's Bible as a girl, often admiring those I was supposed to abhor—something about the strong lines of Jezebel's back as she waited to be pushed from her tower to the waiting dogs below. Such pluck—the way she painted her face even as they came for her. Those biblical temptresses, what sway they held in a time of men who parted rivers and stared down lions, what rare and delicious power. Delilah and Eve and Bathsheba. Later Salome and Mary Magdalene. All of them, really. Except Sarah.

Wife to Abraham, Sarah could bear no children and, at her suggestion, Abraham made a child with their servant, Hagar. This was perhaps odd, but mostly fine, until Sarah, at the age of ninety, made a covenant with God and bore Abraham a second son. Then the real trouble began. The sight of Hagar with her child became a thorn to Sarah once her arms were filled with a child of her own. She began to nag and moan until, at her insistence, Abraham banished Hagar and his firstborn son. I can still see the Bible's illustration: Hagar dark-skinned and huddled with her boy, Sarah's pale arms crossed, her mouth sour as Abraham points a finger in a southerly direction.

It's possible that the olive trees in Lebanon were not around at the time of Noah. Perhaps they came later. Perhaps Sarah herself gave root to the famous trees. They may have sprouted from pits tossed from a platter at her baby shower, a ninety-year-old oohing over the ancient equivalents of receiving blankets and baby oil, so delighted that, in a fit of happiness, she threw the olive pits behind the party tent. Lush as a new river, that Sarah, walking around her hut like a movie star, wearing her fertility like a gold sticker placed upon her wizened forehead by the hand of God.

But our party was in western New York, not Lebanon. We had no dove, no Noah to warn and save the world from deluge. Even if the party hall were an ark, it had anchored itself along a suburban stretch of lawn, the tree near its door not an olive, but a magnolia. Still, magnolias are an ancient genus, millions of years old; the trees existed even before bees and had to rely on beetles for pollination. Beetles are sloppy as tanks when it comes to the task, sometimes chewing petals in place of the pollen and as a result, the magnolia, despite its elegant appearance, is in fact a rugged bloom, more primitive than olive trees and Sarah and maybe even love.

Inside the party hall, the sound of music and laughter.

Nineteen ninety-six. There would have been Eric Clapton and Blues Traveler for my husband. Barenaked Ladies and Alanis Morissette for my sister. The Weather Girls and ABBA for our friend—and for all of us really, because who could stand still to "Dancing Queen"? Friends danced in groups. Couples danced in pairs. Slow drags. My husband danced with another man. Gay or straight, everyone danced whatever way they wanted, so much movement blurring the edges of the evening I'm not sure whether I danced with my husband to "I Fall to Pieces," or only imagined it later—but no, I was busy walking someone's uncle to the door, someone not keen on male-on-male dancing, who'd waited an appropriate amount of time before announcing his departure.

"Good-bye," he said and walked out into the night. "Thank you," he said. "So sorry to have to go," by which he meant that the cake and the music were fine but he could not abide the sight of men slow-dragging to Patsy Cline. It was a tiny loss, his leaving, the door opening to usher him out into a night that had already begun to grow cold.

The cakes were specially ordered. Made by a friend of a friend, a man who had a way with flour and sugar. Beautiful things. Frothy as ballerinas, perfect as debutantes. Hazelnut maybe, rich chocolate, one of them flavored with raspberry liqueur and whipped cream. And, as if it were a wedding and not a birthday celebration, the cakes were given the honor of their own table, a space more magnetic than even the gift table. The cakes were like hearts beating atop a tablecloth and I wanted more than anything to push my fingers into the pink one and lift it in frosted sections to my mouth. But I contained myself. My husband was turning thirty. As was my sister and my friend, whose mother stood and sang. She had a voice like old times, his mother. Big band and straight whiskey. A voice like crushed velvet. Everyone dancing, everyone forgetting the world while we could.

Look back and such nights thicken with metaphor. The magnolia must symbolize fruit and bloom and possibility. The snow stands, of course, for unexpected turns in the weather. And the drink in my hand? The way I brought it to my lips as the snow began to fall—is that a stand-in for freedom or despair?

I was new to drinking. I'd gone through the motions, but never really let myself go. I'd held off because of a grandmother's sloshed calls from the West Coast, her diatribes coming without regard to differences in time zone or the motion of our lives. She discovered where we went to church and placed drunken calls to the priest, the wet accusations and sloppy confessions—the shame of it all, a grandmother disturbing the peace, a grandmother engaging in bar fights, then calling a stranger thousands of miles away for absolution. How much I wanted a grandmother who crocheted soft things instead of one who nursed a black eye with a T-bone like something out of a cartoon, one whose death came when her body could no longer sustain the ongoing assault. *Cirrhosis.* Even the word was ugly. And the men in my old neighborhood, holding court on street corners with their brown bags of liquor and bloated words, making little kingdoms with their longing.

Given such examples, I'd avoided anything stronger than wine or the frilliest of drinks, still believing, at least in part, in rewards for good behavior, allowing myself only a time or two of overindulgence. But on that night goodness itself felt like a lie so I let myself taste it, the way it dismantled the angles, the way it blotted. We were in our twenties, three of us turning thirty—what would have been in our cups? Rum perhaps, or fruit juice mixed with vodka. Drinks poured from a shaker and topped with cherries, something hard and certain and sweet.

I should have known his hands by then, they were always too big and too cold. I'd have normally avoided a doctor's appointment on the day of a party, but it was an emergency. While it's possible the doctor I'd had since I was a teenager only put his hands on top of me, I remember his hands inside me in spite of the seed growing and how tender, but he examined my body and shook his head, considering the few drops of blood that had brought me to him.

"Well, you still feel a little pregnant," he said, sizing up the state of my life with one hand while turning toward the sink.

I sat on the table, trying to keep the paper gown from falling apart, unsure of whether to be glad I was still pregnant, if only just a little, or to give in to the desire to crumple to the floor. I thought of the party, the work to do, the way I'd begun to see Paul as a father— the pair of old-fashioned Keds I'd given him because they seemed the sort Ward Cleaver would wear. It was then that I knew. As I sat draped in paper watching the doctor write on my chart. *A little pregnant.* The way he avoided my eye, the thoroughness with which he washed his hands. I thought of all the years I'd seen him, the way his mildness was less a result of warmth than waxy detachment. The way he performed abortions on the same weekends he delivered babies. The way he'd go about his day either way. There was nothing to justify my flare of anger, no logic or consistency of theme, but it rendered me solid enough to push off the examination table toward the pile of clothes folded on the chair and all that needed doing for the coming night.

And the night came. A party with cakes beating like hearts and someone's mother singing and people rushing to the door, mouths opening like new flowers, running onto wet grass and lifting their hands to the sky, as if it were the first time in the history of the world it had ever snowed.

Blackberry Winter, it's called, a cold spell that follows you into spring, coming after the brambles have blossomed. The opposite of Indian Summer, a blackberry winter takes its name from whatever happens to be blooming when the unexpected cold snap arrives: *Dogwood Winter* when the dogwoods show, *Locust Winter* when the locust flowers are out. *Magnolia Winter,* I suppose, when the snow comes just as a little tree outside a party hall has just shaken its first blossoms awake. An *Olive Winter,* had a light snow fallen onto tiny blossoms in Canaan while Sarah watched her son look up at the sky, the white coming down, the woman, now a hundred years old, wondering how much longer she'd be around to watch him grow.

An olive tree can produce fruit for thousands of years. Pistachios can live for several hundred. Some apple trees go on bearing for more than a hundred years. But a woman is not a fruit tree and, unless she's Sarah from the Bible, has only a few decades in which to reproduce. We are elevated in many ways—walking about on two legs, looking into mirrors, berating ourselves for shortcomings, performing ablutions, and eventually loving ourselves, little goddesses stringing bits of metal and rock round our necks. But compared to the bristlecone pine, we are ants. Compared to the Olive Trees of Noah, our time of bearing is the equivalent of a cigarette break.

It was late when the flood began. The door opened and closed, bringing in gusts of cold as the party whittled down to the closest friends and the most devoted few. It was not dramatic, this deluge; I simply slipped into the bathroom and stayed in one of the stalls while people left in groups, laughing as they went out into the snow. I waited for the silence that told me everyone had gone, but instead someone came to find me. Paul, I suppose, though I begged him not to tell. A few had seen me with a drink earlier, staring out the window, and saying, *Are you sure you should be drinking that?* Yes, I said, I'm sure. Because by then, I knew. And all that was left was the strange fact of snow on magnolia petals.

The next day it was as if it had rained inside my body, as if the entirety of Noah's flood, forty days and forty nights, had been waiting under the skin, pooled and swollen, and had finally broken loose. I'd cradled the telephone all night, drifting off between rings, the doctor on call checking in. "It's me," he said, like he was my oldest friend in the world, and on that night maybe he was. I slept in the guest room to keep Paul from the mess of trips to the bathroom, and I suppose I'd cultivated by then a preference for bearing things alone—or else I was testing him, saying, *I'll be better on my own,* and flunking him when he said *okay* too quickly or flunking myself for lying in the first place—all of this while holding onto the phone.

"Everything will be fine," the doctor said, "you're doing just fine."

"Yes," I said, agreeing that I was doing fine when, in fact, I was doing nothing but yielding to the work of my body. "Okay," I said when he called to remind me to see my doctor first thing. "I promise," I said to the voice that came one last time as the sun rose, then fell away like an old sweater I'd needed on a chilly night long ago.

The sun was out. Everything was light. A proper May. Except for a few fallen blossoms, no one would have known how cold it had been just a few hours before, the snow falling and melting while most people slept.

What the Body Wants

WHEN SHE'S BORN, A girl is lousy with eggs. Like a clownfish or a cod, all those follicles waiting to rise and flare. By puberty only a quarter of the original two million remain and in her lifetime, only four hundred follicles will mature into ripened eggs. Four hundred chances for things to line up just right, for the moon of her ovum to burgeon and divide into another of her kind.

Trying to force the body to bear fruit isn't as pretty as forcing forsythia in winter, not as simple as submerging cut branches into warm water to trick them into flowering. The body is not a shrub. There's no getting around its particular vocabulary. When you force the body, words like *follicle stimulating hormone* (FSH) and *human chorionic gonadotropic* (HCG) and *luteinizing hormone* (LH) enter your life. It's a return to grade school with a new list of vocabulary words to learn. Nothing so lovely as an eruption of yellow in mid-March. Except that forsythia contain ovaries too, and have their own lexicon. A fact to keep in mind as you find the spot on your thigh and jab the needle hard and fast. Too shallow and you'll miss the muscle and have to try again. Too deep and the spot will sting for days. It's understandable then, isn't it, the desire to memorize instead the language of flowers? *Stigma* and *style*. *Sepal* and *calyx*. *Petal* and *corolla*.

Mine is not called a *Fertility Clinic*. It's called a *Center for Reproductive Endocrinology*, which sounds better somehow—less Movie of the Week and more medically valid—but still amounts to a brochure rack loaded with information on in vitro fertilization and sperm washing. No matter what it's called, the waiting room is populated by women whose bodies are straight and tall or round and short, women with older partners or female partners or no partners, women past typical childbearing age, and a few like me, under thirty—all of us flipping through magazines with smiling women and beautiful homes on their covers. A room occupied by those waiting to discuss the progress of their cycles, women awaiting the results of blood tests to measure FSH levels, couples with brown bags waiting for their artificial insemination appointments, women biting the insides of their lips while listening for their names to be called, all looking and not looking at the door to the inner sanctum of the examination rooms, a door plastered with photographs of babies, all pink and clean and new, twins overrepresented. The one thing everyone has in common, besides waiting, is the way our eyes travel to and from that door, the way we pick up and put down again the home and garden magazines, study the framed artwork and the brochure rack, shift in our seats, trying to hide the fear that the follicles didn't develop or the blood test will be negative—all under the watch of a squadron of beautiful babies.

The serum injected into the thigh is a purified form of FSH extracted from human urine. "From postmenopausal women," my doctor says, and while I'm absorbing this fact, she adds, "from nuns."

Nuns from Italy, it turns out.

FSH is the hormone responsible for the development of egg follicles and rises in women after menopause so that, ironically, women no longer able to bear children produce in excess exactly what's needed to ovulate and become pregnant. A fact that resulted in kindly older women donating their urine to help strangers halfway across the globe.

I think of this sometimes, in the lab, the exam room, under the glare of all the tubes and machines and lights—those nuns sharing their pee for the making of babies they will never hold. How strange this world, so advanced and so wonderfully primitive.

From our beginnings, humans have done what we could to trick the earth into giving up its riches. We perform rituals to fatten the crops, offer blessings to enhance our offspring, and create figures like the twenty-five-thousand-year-old Venus of Willendorf with her red ochre tinted belly to cultivate fertility in times of famine. So many symbols, so many hopeful acts. The club-wielding Cerne Abbas Giant, a naked figure drawn onto a hill in the English countryside, was said to help childless couples who danced around or slept on the site to improve their chances for conception. In the city of Amarante, pastries are shaped into phalluses and named for São Gonçalo, Portugal's patron saint of love. We sacrifice chickens; throw rice at weddings; rub bellies against coffins; fashion maypoles from birch maypoles; tattoo trees onto brides' foreheads; press turmeric—and sometimes coriander and saffron—onto the bodies of new couples; pour water over the heads of girls at Easter; sip teas made with bits of sparrow and hare; and touch the trousers on the statue of Victor Noir in Père Lachaise Cemetery, kiss him softly on the lips, and place a flower in his stone hat. Some carry hazelnuts and jasmine flowers; have sex in farmers' fields; whip girls with willow branches; place a thumb in the column of St. Gregory in Istanbul; float wreaths of flowers in rivers; walk in the shadow of a lusty woman; jump bonfires; pray novenas to St. Brigit of Kildare, St. Gerard Majella, and St. Rita of Cascia; and pass through an ancient stone hole backward on the night of a full moon.

My counselor said it was my second chakra. "The Swadhisthana Chakra."
Though I tend to be cynical where chakras are concerned, I was so tired of focusing on my ovaries I'd begun to hate the very word.

Ovary. How medical it sounded, how naked and how slippery. The idea of contemplating a lotus was a relative relief.

"The chakra is aligned with reproduction, but also with unconscious desires and creativity," the counselor said.

I fixed my gaze on the box of Kleenex kept on the side table for those who came before and after me, men and women who sat in the very same seat discussing troubled marriages and alcoholism and thwarted dreams. I stared into the Kleenex, rolling my eyes while trying to hide how much I wanted to believe in chakras and lotus blossoms.

"It's as though you are stuck in many ways," he said. "Where else aren't you freed up creatively?"

He'd been my counselor for years. I knew he was right for me when, years earlier, we'd felt the earth shake during a session and ran to the window to see what caused the boom. Barnum & Bailey, it turned out; the circus was parading into town, their elephants thundering down city streets. It seemed a sign. There were others. When I took a fringed pillow from the end of the small sofa and held it up to block my eyes during my first few sessions, he never once suggested I put it down. When I complained about the fertility drugs making me fat, he only offered me a Buddha smile and said, "Some people get bigger when big things are about to happen."

"What a lie," I thought. "What a perfectly gorgeous lie."

Now he was talking chakras and creativity and other ways in which I might be stuck. I must have snarled and made a crack about needing to make a painting of goldfinches to jump-start my ovaries, but eventually, my shoulders would have relaxed as I breathed, allowing myself to conjure a lotus and imagine it unfold one vermilion petal at a time.

The Internet was still new in the mid-'90s but was already organizing itself into websites and discussion groups and topic-related listservs. I researched as much as I could about the world within my body, trying to make sense of the stew of hormones, reading books and articles and websites where people shared theories about special diets, medical treatments, and specialists. One name kept coming up. An expert. A real life fertility god. One who, it turned out, would spend an hour online answering questions during an upcoming chat session. *Oh my god*, women with handles such as W8N4BABY and H4PPYM4M4 wrote about the upcoming session: *I can't wait!*

Women all over the country plugged in, posing questions about selective reduction, blighted ova, and intrauterine insemination. The expert may have sat in a den in Iowa wearing a T-shirt and faded Levi's. He may have been in an office in New York, wearing a suit jacket and loosened tie. He may have been in his bedroom in Montreal, a tangle of underwear and back hair, but I imagined him in a white coat seated beside an examination table, hands in latex gloves. Back and forth the questions and answers came, until finally there was an opening. I was shy, even online, but eager, and began typing my question.

Sometimes I feel pain in the sides of my pelvis—my fingers shook as if I were posing my question to an actual god—*near my ovaries, almost as if they want to ovulate.*

I hit "send" as fast as I could, before another woman's question could appear on the screen and steal his attention. Before I could write a follow-up to ask why the pain might be coming, or what it might mean, his answer flashed back from Iowa or Montreal or New York: *Ovaries are organs. They don't WANT anything.*

Why, then, the pregnancy tests bought in bulk? Why so much time spent sitting on the edge of the tub and toilet lid waiting for pink lines and plus signs to appear? Why the slow tick of timer and the looking away from the little window *because a watched pot never boils*? Why the counting of tiles in the shower and the staring into my bent reflection in the faucet? Why the half-moon shapes of fingernails pushed into the palms? *Two lines for positive, one for negative.* Why the heaviness when the second line doesn't appear? The closing of eyes? The long washing of hands to delay relaying failure to the one waiting outside the door? Why the cursing and crying, the brave faces and telling ourselves we'll have better luck next time?

Some say elevating the legs is useless, but I was a devotee. After shooting myself up and having my blood drawn—each possibility for life monitored and measured, after hearing the doctor say, *We have a good one here, so go home and get busy*, about the act with my husband that had once meant something else—after all that, I wasn't taking any chances.

I'd prop my body atop a pillow, point my legs to the ceiling, dreaming up a parade of womb-shaped things, letting them pass before me—mangoes, avocados, and pears, of course; bleached deer skulls from O'Keeffe paintings; light bulbs; certain knots in certain trees; the Toyota logo; bicycle handlebars when viewed head on; the blue swirls of a wallpaper from some long-ago room. I'd imagine meadows of poppies in bloom or conjure a flock of elderly virgins half a world away, the good Sisters, *buone Suore*, smiling at me, wishing me luck. I made the ceiling into a projector, saying *no thank you* when Paul asked if I wanted company while counting down the minutes. I told myself I was being kind when I said *no*, freeing him when he wanted to go, but the truth is that I was selfish in my grief but also in my hope, keeping for myself the expanse of white paint while holding my body in an upside-down pirouette.

Meiosis. Mitosis. Cellular division. The girl across from me has hair like gold and the boy beside me smells like cut grass. The word *tawny* could be used to describe the hair, the word *pastoral* to describe the scent. My lab partners in college biology class. We're supposed to be sketching the various phases of cellular division, but the boy makes jokes and something about the girl reminds me of Rachel Ward in *The Thorn Birds* so that I expect Richard Chamberlain as Father de Bricassart to stroll into the classroom. But the biology professor is the only one to stroll by. We laugh and scratch something onto our papers, marks made and forgotten as soon as class is over. Which may explain why I never mastered the subject of reproduction, and why, to me, cellular division is the scent of newly mown lawns and Rachel Ward playing Meggie Cleary on an Australian beach, setting a hibiscus in her hair and pushing bare feet through the sand while waiting for her true love to arrive.

Sterile is a scalpel of a word. *Barren* makes a woman into a hillside where not even the bristly sedge will grow. *Infertile* is not correct because women bear fruit in ways beyond the womb. But we need a word, don't we, for those times when the organs and the slush of hormones fail to negotiate the precise requirements needed to spark and sustain procreation? What to call it then? This resistance of the flesh, this thwarting of a process taken for granted, this inability to master the most basic of cellular activities. Come up with a word that says I'm unsure about what it means to be fruitful. Label my chemistry overly sensitive. Name my rising ambivalence with a cognate of Latin that means *occasionally half hearted*. Say my chakras are in need of alignment. Touch me with anything but a scalpel. Call me anything but a brown hill.

I began to dream of finding babies. In overgrown lots. Stashed inside bathroom stalls at work, swaddled and lying in playgrounds. One appeared in the kitchen sink, all wet smiles and cooing as she floated between coffee mugs and cereal bowls. Mostly, though, they were desperate dreams and therefore given to cliché—babies left on church steps, the arriving priest finding the precious package and deciding on me as the perfect mother. The baby was a boy. The baby was a girl. A little pink bundle. A perfect weight of soft brown skin settling into my arms. An infant floating like Moses in a basket patched with tar and pitch hidden among the bulrushes. A gift from the river. A child offered up. A perfect baby waiting, just waiting, to be found.

Sometimes there is a God and two lines appear in the window of the plastic stick. You check and check again and yes, it's still there, and birds swell in the sky of your chest. So many wings beating at once, starlings rising from the branches of a sugar maple, as if the tree itself has lifted into flight. A flock of starlings is called a *murmuration* and the word perfectly describes the feeling of two lines coming together on the pregnancy test—so many birds rising at once.

Say a woman is more than the sum of her parts and I'll listen. Say that she is more than fruit and blossom and branch and I'll nod my head *yes*. But say the body does not want and I will fall to the floor under the weight of a world that does not heed the sweet talk of a heartbeat.

Of course the body wants. It wants to pump blood. It longs for the chest to fill with breath, for the breath to be held a perfect interval then released back into the world. It wants to flex muscle. It wants to touch the shape of a song with the perfect shell of its ear. It wants to move toward other bodies, wishes it could push past walls of membrane and tissue and settle for a while into the impossible home of the other. Just as a plant bends its green toward the sun, the body is a field of pulsing chlorophyll, all stem and flower and root. It wants to turn over its shadowy blue cells while humming to the music of its own movement, to stretch and grow, to continue in its particular splendor.

Our Lady of the Roses

HERE I AM.

Crouched in the space between kitchen and living room, my voice swelling with pride as I speak my words into the phone. My words. Just two. *I'm pregnant.* I turn my head from my husband as I speak. He's on the sofa, a few feet away, and I'm shy about the way my happiness spills from me. And really there's no time to worry over such matters because my mother has something to say, her own bit of news to share. Her whisper is giddy. My mother is in her late fifties, but the voice coming through the phone is a six-year-old who's just stolen a sweet from the cupboard.

"You're not going to believe this," she says.

I steady my breath. There's no telling what will come out of my mother's mouth, but I breathe deeply and try to convince myself that I'm years of therapy past the point of disbelief.

"I'm pregnant too." Her voice is high and full, and cut only by the sound of cheering. I can see with a bend of my head that the clapping is for the ballgame Paul has flicked on, but it sounds as if the cheering is for my mother and her big news.

"I'm pregnant too," she repeats and I push as far as the telephone cord will let me, farther from the television and the sound of cheering.

"What?" My voice cracks. Therapy is overrated because she was right; I cannot believe it.

"I'm going to have a baby," she says.

"But . . . that's impossible." My voice is hard, a pebble against the expanse of my mother's sky. She turned fifty-eight back in January, and apart from a preference for black raspberry ice cream and the tendency to freckle in summer, January birthdays are the only thing we have in common.

Until tonight. Now, it seems, we are both mothers-to-be.

"I know," she's chuckling as if explaining a lottery win to a local reporter. "But I've always been so fertile. One look at a man and poof, I'm pregnant."

I squelch the desire to remind her that she does more than look while wondering whether she's just sloppy in her excitement or if her easy fertility has been pointed out on purpose. Either way, she doesn't seem to recall that I've spent the last year undergoing treatment accessing parts of my body I didn't know existed, and it doesn't matter, because the fact is this: my mother is a ripened tree, an avocado clustered with glossy fruit holding court over a small Mexican square.

She's laughing now, saying she's told no one. Not even her husband. "But with you sharing your news," she says, "how could I keep this to myself?"

I look into the other room. Paul is tuned into the game. This may be because he heard me pick up the phone to dial my mother and knows such calls to be punctuated by fits of chocolate and swearing or because the Phillies are playing and the game is good.

Probably the latter. Paul is not complex.

"You would not believe how thick my hair is right now, and one look at boiled chicken and I can't keep a thing down." Now my mother is listing her symptoms. Now she's my best girlfriend, grieving over sore breasts and tight waistbands. She doesn't ask how it happened. My magic. And I don't tell her that this time feels different. I don't say that this time I allow myself to collect tiny T-shirts and soft white pieces of cloth I store in the back of the closet and take out when I'm alone.

She does not ask and I do not tell. My mother prefers to speak of pleasant things and besides, this call I've made to south Texas has turned so fully on its side that I've almost forgotten my news as she talks now about missed periods, how she hasn't had one in over four months.

"And I've always been so regular," she's saying. "Every twenty-eight days, steady as the moon."

She can't be pregnant. I think of my six siblings and the child that was stillborn before most of us came. My mother has had eight full-term pregnancies, I remind myself, so she ought to know. If it were not for the limitations of time and gestation, she would have churned out a hundred children by now. I cover my face with my free hand, imagining a shared baby shower, the competing pile of presents, her wide grin as she opens a package of burping cloths.

I look at my husband to squelch the scene. Paul's on the sofa, face turned toward the game so that I'm left with only a head of hair the color of straw and a view of a uniformed man on TV. The batter is on the plate, scraping his feet against the earth like a bull, making circular movements with his body.

"The strange thing," my mother says—I'm still digesting her news but secure in my belief that nothing could be stranger. The man on TV winds at the plate, making the whole of his body into an extension of the bat—"The strange thing," she says again, lowering her voice, "is that Joe and I haven't had sex in awhile."

The man on the screen holds the bat so tightly it looks as though the wood might fly apart. He's waiting for the pitcher to let loose, tracing circles into the sky with the tip of his Louisville Slugger.

"What's *awhile*?" I ask, turning back into the call. "How long?"

"I don't know." She's a child again. "Maybe six months."

I almost feel the crack of bat breaking ball, as the sound of the television explodes. I turn to see the crowd is on its feet, gone crazy over the out. The Phillies must be playing in Atlanta because the crowd wears war paint and makes chopping motions with the tomahawks of their arms. They do their chant, their mock Indian chant, and I find myself wanting to melt into the television screen where I might join them and make a tomahawk of my arm.

Instead, I straighten my back and turn from the game. She hasn't had sex since before the missed periods, I think; well then, that's it.

"Okay," I say. "It must be menopause."

The silence on her end tells me she's offended by the very suggestion.

"All women go through menopause," I say, suddenly taking on the role of a supportive daughter in a Lifetime movie for women. *Mother-Daughter Body Talk*, it would be called, or *Menopause Moment*.

Only my mother's not buying it. She's *not* everyone. Hasn't she spent years convincing us both of that?

"I know the signs," she says, voice chilly.

I shake my head and lean into the call. "I've had a pregnancy test," I say. "Have you?"

"No," she answers flatly, disgusted by the sterility of my suggestion. "I don't need a doctor to tell me about my own damned body." She's annoyed. The notion that she requires intercourse to become pregnant seems limiting to her, fun spoiling. Like someone admitting they're using a hand to push the heart-shaped piece of wood along the surface of the Ouija board.

"I've done this many times," she says, "and it's always the same, the puffiness in my face, the swelling of my belly, the sharpened sense of smell . . ."

"But Ma, if you haven't had sex . . ." I look to the sofa. Despite the pairing of the words "ma" and "sex," the fine blond head does not move.

"When was the last time you saw a doctor?" I ask, but she interrupts.

"It's happened before, you know." There's something new on her end of the line. Something expectant and so full it breaks apart in my ears. Her voice is shooting stars, all glitter and shine, and I know by the shimmer of her words and this new quality in her voice that she's referring to Mary. Jesus and Mary. Or Sarah from the Bible, her post-menopausal body made fruitful after a covenant with God.

It's happened before, you know.

A knot begins in my stomach. I know this woman, my mother, is given to flights of fancy and will always prefer a Hollywood-style miracle over the cool scalpel of logic; still, I swallow hard, pushing a hand through my hair.

"What do you mean?" I say, my voice becoming a knife. "As in the *Virgin Mary?*"

Her silence is all the answer I need. I see her face on a tabloid then, the headline rising before me: SOUTH TEXAS SENIOR PREGNANT BY GOD. I imagine the way I'll have to explain to friends, *she just gets carried away sometimes.*

She stays quiet and I'm somewhere between guilty that I've ruined her news, envious over a fertility so lush it doesn't require intercourse, and ashamed that I have a mother who not only believes in pregnancy without copulation but practices it.

But then I remember a friend's mother whose belly swelled with tumor when she got sick, whose cancer mimicked the signs of pregnancy in the months before she died.

"Ma," I say, "you have to see a doctor."

And there's just enough space before she speaks so that I think maybe she's heard. But no.

"I'll talk to the priest this Sunday after Mass," she finally whispers, and I know she doesn't intend to get advice so much as to secure his backing on the possibility of biblical-style conception. I imagine the poor padre trying to pick his way through a conversation with my mother, who will cause more grief over her condition than the most inspired pilgrim in his flock. She will test the man's faith. She will not see a doctor. And I know of no way to sway her.

Instead I consider chucking something at the body on the sofa. I want to throw Paul a look that says *help me, you shit, my mother thinks she's pregnant by God.* But even with all the expressive power at my disposal, I have no access to looks that make such statements. I think back to when we first started trying, when Paul had to give a sample to make sure all was right on his side. A private person and a Protestant to begin with, he'd hated the functionless sexuality of the task and stood straight-backed, resisting, while I'd ranted over his stubborn timidity, saying no wonder I wasn't pregnant and crying over how very wrong and broken everything was.

When he finally submitted and the doctors declared him fit, confirming that the problem was mine, I began sticking myself with needles and propping my legs skyward until finally I was pregnant and Paul looked somehow redeemed; and despite our losses, we kept trying and sometimes winning so that I'd allowed myself the collection of soft white things and kept my secret safe for the prescribed amount of time. Until this moment. Until this phone call.

Which is where we are.

Me, wondering how to snare my husband's attention with a loose potholder or a shoe, but knowing that certain attentions can't be demanded. Paul sprawled out on the sofa watching players running toward well-marked goals in a game five states away.

Here I am. Sitting on a strip of carpet listening to my mother rise into happiness again. Only this time I stop talking. I let her words come and decide to receive them without the cruelty of common sense. And in my quiet the image of my mother is transformed. She becomes clearer, without the muddle of words. She's no longer a woman sitting in the cracked chair of a kitchenette, white hair newly cropped, something growing in her body she can't yet name. Instead, she's part of the night sky, my mother. Cloaked in a blue-green mantle, light spilling from her in jagged angles, surrounding her body in a wash of gold. Now my mother is *Nuestra Señora*, bare feet set upon a sliver of moon, angels gathered round, mouth bent in satisfaction.

I close my eyes as she speaks and imagine roses opening from her fingertips as she moves once again into a steady stream of chatter, her voice finding the cushion of my ear as she nurses her pregnancy myth. Together we avoid the obvious. Together we enter into a collusion of foolishness, the best sort of kindness we have. I listen as my mother tells the story of her many labors, trying my best to keep sight of the pink petals as they open around her, almost managing a smile as she tells me of her plans to scour the thrift shops of Brownsville for a crib.

Time will pass. My mother will see a doctor when she no longer has a choice. All talk of babies will have stopped by then—will have stopped, in fact, after that first phone call. There will be nothing so ordinary or miraculous for either of us, and it turns out that we were both delusional in our own way. Later, she'll say the weeks she spends in Houston are tough not so much for the cancer treatment she undergoes but because until then she's never spent a night alone. I will hear the fear in her voice and think of my own nights, the way my solitude feels sweeter than it should. She may hear the catch in my voice and wonder what kind of woman wants to sleep alone when there's an offer to share her bed. I will do my best and so will she, and the phone calls will stop coming until they come again— for we will always be partners in some things, my mother and I, and strangers in others.

Sybil

IT'S POSSIBLE THAT WHEN he called me *Sybil*, he didn't mean the woman with sixteen personalities. He may not have meant the character played by Sally Field in the 1970s television miniseries, though her name had become a sort of cultural shorthand for spastic changes in personality and he did have a thing for Sally Field, especially in her *Norma Rae* days. I'd always been prone to shifting moods, but was especially temperamental in those days, my spirits rising and falling within the space of five minutes, spinning and flapping, moving from soft to raging without pattern or provocation, so he must have meant the TV Sybil. Still, the unconscious has its powers so that perhaps without realizing it my husband was invoking the title given to female mystics in the classical world. *Sybils* they were called, women populating ancient temples and sanctuaries, speaking their riddled truths and channeling the divine, including at Delphi, where the Oracle sat upon a fissure in the earth spouting her wisdom in a fevered rush.

We'd been to Delphi on a trip to Greece the year before and maybe he'd remembered stories of the sybils. Perhaps he'd seen signs of possession, recognizing before I did the prophecy in my frenzies.

The doctor wore the sort of clogs normally sported by certain unfussy women. His precise movements and German accent lent him a semirobotic quality as he instructed me to insert the tip of the ultrasound transducer into my body—it was a sort of etiquette, I'd noticed, allowing the patient to insert the probe before the doctor took hold of the handle and navigated it around her pelvis. We'd look without speaking at the images that filled the screen, all shadowy outline and murky striation, repeating the procedure several times a week for months at a time. It was odd, yes, though the doctor softened after a few months. During the visit when I confessed to praying for a miracle at Delphi, he forgot himself and touched me, human-like, something about the Oracle or the desperation of admitting prayer melting him.

"You will have your miracle," he said—a promise I'd never hold him to, but how kind such promises sometimes. The sudden flush of warmth after so much coolness spun my head, but even this could not make the transducer appointments less awkward.

The strangest thing was the latex glove slid onto the probe before it was inserted into the body. To keep it sterile, I suppose, and maybe surgical gloves were easier to come by than condoms, and with less troublesome associations. Or perhaps it was only the fact that gloves didn't require individual unwrapping. Either way, a glove went onto the tip of the ultrasound probe—but a probe is a probe and not a hand, and only one finger was needed to sheath it. The other four fingers flapped to the side. The first time it was held out to me, the transducer with its slackened latex fingers, I measured the distance to the door with my eyes, wondering how many steps it would take to escape. By the time I was done I'd seen more images of my reproductive system than of my relatives, and modesty was a long-gone luxury. In the beginning, though, there was only the shock and the decision to stay put, doing what I could to pretend the probe was a wand, imagining the flattened fingers rising up to wave a tiny hello as they entered my body.

He's a magician, I told myself, *a holy man*, remembering the Sanctuary at Delphi, picturing lemon groves and marble columns as my reproductive universe lit up on the screen and we tracked the progress of my ovum like the movement of the moon in the night sky, watching over it, using salves and potions, and doing whatever was necessary to make it fatten and bloom.

The ancient Greeks believed Delphi to be center of the earth. Zeus sent two eagles flying in opposite directions and their paths crossed at the site, which became known as the *omphalos*, the navel of the earth. It was marked with a sacred stone and was originally guarded by the serpent, Python, which is why the sybil there was called Pythia. The most important prophet in the classical world, she was also known as the Oracle and was consulted by warriors and kings on everything from battle plans to matters of the heart.

The Oracle sat on a tripod over an opening in the earth where the slain serpent's body released vapors that sent her into a trance. Intoxicated, the sybil could better tune into the words of Apollo and speak them as she sat draped in a scarlet robe and swaying upon her three-legged throne. Pilgrims came offering laurel wreaths and carrying goats for sacrifice. They came, full of hope and tired from walking, putting their questions to her and waiting as the riddles she spoke were combed for truth.

I hadn't lied to the German doctor. I had stood at Mt. Parnassus looking into a valley ripe with olive groves and whitewashed country houses in something close to prayer.

We were based in Athens, which was dark with the hungry eyes of newly arrived Eastern European prostitutes, flies crowding stalls, and freshly slaughtered animals hanging in shops. Beautiful ruins around every turn, black coffee and sweetshops on every corner, and the orthodox priests with their vigorous beards, but there was no time in Athens when we weren't plagued by stray dogs. Even on the islands—where we found pistachio groves and citrus trees, water so blue it hurt to look, late night meals of retsina and cheese—there were strays everywhere. Cats skulked in the shade of old windmills, their numbers multiplying with each glance—black cats on white-tiled terraces, tortoiseshells curled near the entry to cafés, kittens batting insects under olive trees. The cats couldn't hop ferries or fishing boats to the mainland and had no choice but to stay in paradise making more of themselves.

But at Delphi, the air was clear and fine, the scent of cypress combined with the sound of birds, so I stopped and made myself quiet. It was not a formal prayer. I did not fold my hands or make requests so much as breathe in the trees while feeling myself open to the largeness of things while laying down my desire like an offering to the gods. And why not? If the earth were a woman, Delphi would be her belly button—the place itself took its name from the same root as *delphys*, the Greek word for womb.

Sybil of the book who spawned the television miniseries claimed to have sixteen distinct personalities taking turns with her body. One or two talked with baby voices. One was a boy skilled at carpentry. Another displayed an intense fear of Roman Catholics. A sophisticated blonde spoke French and another young lady played piano. Each personality seemed to have its specialty, so that I couldn't help but envy the way they all chipped in. Still, sixteen is a heaping spoonful when it comes to personalities—but if I'm honest about my desire to become a mother, I have to admit I was of at least as many minds.

Years before I'd known a man whose apartment was so hot in summer we slept near the window and took turns dousing each other with a spray bottle. Bouts of love followed by sections of cantaloupe and lazy drowsing, but mostly our bodies at work before the open window. I woke from a fit of sleep once, a word fixed in my head. I'd dreamt words before, but this one I didn't know. *Fecundity.* I said it aloud and asked the man who scowled at the idea of dreaming unknown words, but finally, he answered, saying it meant fertility, a certain richness in women and plants. *A fine word, don't you think?* He became philosophical as he thought of it, wanting to discuss the slow curve of certain letters, the way some words pulse under the surface of things, how we occasionally forget all that we know.

I have to go, I said, citing the heat, and he—who did not normally risk expression except when it came breakfast, which he liked very much to prepare and to share—he felt acutely alone then and said, *Just this once, stay the night.* I was twenty or so and high on being desired, which rendered me occasionally without mercy. But I stayed, insisting on moving to the floor where I could be alone with the word expanding in me like an overripe pear. *Fecundity.* A cruelty to someone who'd only just made it out of a neighborhood that held its girls not with chains or cuffs but with the babies piled in their laps.

I'd chosen the Man of the Most Generous Breakfasts because of how different he was from the other man, the one from my neighborhood, the one by my side during the talk by the visiting theologian a few weeks prior. We'd sat in the front row, his niece flopped across our laps, her dark curls captivating all who passed—including the theologian, who'd said, *What a beautiful family you have*, when I thanked her for the talk. Something sank in me then. I'd wanted her to see the fire in my eye, not the child in my lap. I loved that young man and his gorgeous niece but wanted nothing to do with what they might mean. Which led to an overheated room and making a bed of the floor while a new word came to unsettle my dreams.

How long to keep trying? The doctors couldn't answer. I asked the German, who'd become so kind by then he only smiled gently and said, "I see no reason why things won't work." How young I was, still thinking the world was made up of answers waiting to be found, as if the solution might be sewn into the inside of a lab coat. I'd heard stories about neighbors or sisters or mothers who were told they'd never carry to term. Always these stories were punctuated with happy endings: "Then, when she'd finally given up any chance, my mother got pregnant and voilà, here I am!"

If there were other stories, of sisters and neighbors and friends who'd stopped trying, women who'd learned to live fully without children, I didn't hear them. Everyone loves a happy ending. Everyone wants to offer hope, so these were the stories people told.

"Audrey Hepburn," someone said, "suffered several miscarriages before having two sons." People brought up Sophia Loren and the actress from *I Dream of Jeannie*. Goddesses of film and screen who'd struggled with pregnancy loss, but who'd persevered and become mothers in the end. One doctor told of a woman with fifteen miscarriages going to full term on her sixteenth try.

"My God," I said, "fifteen times." I let my head fall into my hands as if to show how little I had left.

"But she has a child now," the doctor said. "She never gave up, and now she's a mother."

The nausea came in gigantic waves. I leaned over and threw up in my hands, crying at the mess, resenting the lurching of body, saying, *Why on earth did I do this to myself?* Just once. I'd been sick on several occasions, but had the thought just once. But maybe having such a thought even once was still too much, I wondered later, thinking I'd always said my words too hard.

"You don't know the power of your words," my sister would say when we were kids. She fought with fists while I used my mouth— and it's true that while words came easily, they seemed to me choked and fleeting things and I had no sense of their power. All those prayers said back in high school, the teenager I was having sex without protection, my period late, tears taking the place of breath, moments of high drama, saying, *Please God please God let me not be pregnant let my period come so I can finish high school oh please just this once and I will start showing up on time and doing my homework if you just this once have mercy God O God take pity and let my period come.* Sitting on the edge of my bed, crying into my hands, so certain of my ability to bear children that everything in me played with it like fire, then prayed for its prevention. It's possible that I repeated it once too often, my anti-pregnancy chant, and the words seeped into the fabric of my body, making it into a shield.

I wanted a child, of course I did, but something else was going on as I lifted my legs and stared into the ceiling, imagining his cells as rockets and my egg as moon, visualizing their meeting, coaxing them into collision with the stream of my thoughts.

There was the shock of the body not doing what I'd expected. Failing at what even a twelve-year-old could master. I didn't know one relative or neighbor without her own stories to tell when talk turned to pregnancy and labor. Women had children, plain and simple— the trick to success, it seemed, was to delay it and make it through high school—but that children would come was a given. Pregnancy was as effortless as waking in the morning, as natural as the inhalation of breath. My mother could make a baby as easily as she made biscuits: sifting the flour, adding the salt, using an empty can to cut the dough into perfect circles.

So I became Sybil. Or a sybil. Only instead of unearthing my various personalities or sitting on a fissure over the center of the earth, I stood in the bathroom searching the face in the mirror for signs. It was not an *omphalos*; there was no sweet-smelling stream to send my body into euphoria, no line of priests waiting to make poetry of whatever fell from my mouth. The only marble in sight topped the vanity. There were no columns, no oleander and cypress, no channeling of the divine. Just a young woman in a mirror, looking like someone I recognized, but different somehow, something gone hazy in the eyes.

Then came the day that Paul strode into the bathroom and came out carrying the tray of glass ampules over his head like a waiter at a pizza parlor. He rushed past, long legs pumping toward the trash closet. "This has to stop," he said. "I can't take this anymore."

He opened the door, ready to dump thousands of dollars of fertility drugs into the garbage. I stopped him; whether by laughing or crying, I no longer remember, but I won him over somehow and he apologized, later saying, "Of course we should keep trying." But some things can't be taken back and probably shouldn't be, and while I managed to save the drugs, I couldn't undo the sight of a man whose only weakness was how mild he was trying to dump all that magic and nuns' urine into the trash.

I smiled at my appointments, went along with the injections and blood draws, joking with the phlebotomists, showing up on time—a model patient. But no matter how much I smiled, there were times when a follicle failed to develop, or too many developed, or they developed beautifully but were not fertilized. Failed cycles, they were called, during which one of the doctors said, "We'd achieve better results if we inseminated you here."

It was a cold notion; everything spun and measured under the hum of bright lights. Each time we failed, I'd sit with the doctor who'd prod me to reconsider and each time, I'd resist. Time went on and the doctor pushed a bit more, reminding me of percentages and odds; I knew she was right but I'd politely decline as if she were offering tea instead of processing and placing my husband's semen inside my body.

"Not this time," I said. "No, thank you."

Strange the limits we come to. I'd allow the wand with its ill-fitting glove and slack fingers. I'd allow the bouts of daily blood draws, the injections, the constant monitoring of hormones, the wild flare of body and mood, but would not budge when it came to this.

"Next time," I'd say, and when the next time came, "Just one more try this way."

The doctor would look at me sideways, lips curving playfully at first, then flat-lining and eventually becoming a full-fledged frown. She was nearing the end of her rope. So was I. And it turns out that my desire for a child was not as great as my desire to believe certain things about this life and the ways in which I wanted to go through it.

What would have happened if I'd given in? If I'd held out and tried just one more month? I'll never know because one day I sat there surprised as an ancient Greek seated at the feet of the Oracle at Delphi when a voice rose up from my body and said *no*.

"I'll donate the rest of the drugs," I told the doctor, "but no more."

I'd had enough of pins and needles and the sight of a gentle man gone wild.

Once and for all. No.

I never called them by name. I touched my stomach, of course—a comfort cultivated since childhood, hands tucked into waistband, feeling for the soft pool of flesh. I might have touched with greater purpose, willing something beyond the body to seep into the skin— but I did not even once say to them their names. Never heard them tendered until a friend arranged a Mass and a woman sang a song so sad the entire church became lit with the scent of talcum and someone stood within spitting distance of the Virgin and read the names as though they were lost soldiers. I could only watch as the names were batted about by the flicker of altar candles, floating past the golden doors of the Tabernacle, finding their way to the great panel of stained glass, eventually slipping out into the cold. I stared straight ahead as they sailed away, telling myself they were less like names than seeds from a maple, whirlybirds that hadn't taken to soil. I closed my eyes then to keep what remained of them from falling away like grains of sand in an oyster. For another lifetime perhaps, for the blue undertow of dreams.

How hot and cold I ran in those days, how feverish my wanting, how bitter my disappointment. Silent around most people, at home words tumbled forth. Perhaps I was a sybil. If I could go back and retrace my words, what might wash up in the froth?

The path is never easy, I might have been saying.

Sorry, my dear, but this is not the life for you.

Perhaps the messages weren't so much like fortune cookie wisdom as questions, and if so, what was being asked by the syllables that fell like loose stone from my body?

When was the last time you felt as if of feather?

The last time you felt as if you might float?

What else might it mean, this longing?

I might like to go back. I might like to look again into the eyes of the woman in that mirror; a woman I now see was still a girl. I might like to chew on bay leaves while cloaking myself in scarlet and sitting for a time upon a gilded tripod, listening with new ears to the work of the girl's mouth as she grieves over the body—the futility of pushing them together, the impossibility of breaking them apart. I'd send her patience, perhaps—and kindness—while listening and combing through the scree. Together we'd wait, me on my golden tripod and her standing before the mirror, until the scent of cypress eventually fills the air and a truth rises up from the sound of all the chatter:

Go now from this place. Go now, and see what good might come.

III

What do the pink roses on the fence know of frost?
Of petals scattered like snow?

JUDITH KITCHEN

Flight

THE PROFESSOR STANDS BEFORE us lecturing on family systems, Bowen Theory, and genograms, demonstrating symbols that depict relationships between people—solid lines for marriages, slashes for divorce, a series of dashes and dots for love affairs. "Two circles indicate a trusting relationship," she says, "slashes show discord."

What if children are born out of wedlock? How to show adoption? Physical abuse?

Her answers are solid as the lines between good marriages. She wears a sharp suit, with her dark hair styled just so. Nothing throws her off, no family constellation is too obscure to be taken in and illustrated by the genogram. I sit and listen, but spend most of my time in the back row thawing out.

The walk from the parking lot freezes my face into a mask. I've convinced myself that the drives to and from Buffalo are a return to graduate school, a new beginning, but find as I sit there that I no longer care much for family systems or theories. I rub my hands together while considering my crumbling marriage, the approach of thirty, and what to put into its gaping mouth. I enjoy the drive most of all, the sun sinking into the New York State Thruway, the sky going orange and pink before mottling into darkness—one final burst of light upon metal and glass—so that I'm blinded as I drive west, not seeing where I'm headed exactly but glad at least for movement.

Driving is the best part of everything until the night the professor asks us to write family histories. We'd already used pencils and erasers to make genograms, arriving to class like oversized kindergartners with our drawings—"Now," she says, "we need narratives to accompany them. Write your family stories, going back to before you were born."

I'd barely managed all the slashes and broken lines that was my genogram and slumped under the thought of yet another family tree exercise. They'd come like clockwork each year in grade school, the branches on one side barely filled and those on the other a terrible blank, until I'd finally wised up and learned to lie in sixth grade.

But this is different, I slowly understand, the writing of sentences versus stand-alone names sprouting from Xeroxed branches. The words come with little effort—the logging camps of Maine, the hidden underside of upper New England, all those men dying young, all those hard Yankee women baking pies until they could no longer stand the sight of berries or the little faces gathered in their kitchens.

Something transfers onto the paper as I write, stories so close I'd never really seen them before. It's clear to me suddenly, the way the women in my family are nothing so much as birds, every last one of them throwing herself against cages that seem self-made but are in fact constructed of poverty, early marriage, and children. Each of them doing her best to weather containment until she can take it no more and flies away or lives out her days with an eye perpetually cocked toward open windows.

My days were made of middle schoolers named for exotic flowers and perfume bottles—Amaryllis and Enjoli—girls with eyes so brown and wide I had to look away from time to time lest I fall in; boys with budding muscles who spoke in unguarded moments of the peculiar joy of a basketball as it swishes through a net or the dream of building airplanes and what it might feel like to make something that could lift off the earth.

I kept my job counseling kids who were beautiful and broken and pregnant at thirteen years old, but decided against the PhD and dropped the coursework and the drives to Buffalo. The family history assignment had moved me, but the hook had been the writing, not the theory.

"Take Judy Kitchen's essay workshop," a friend said. She'd suggested it before, swooning over local writers who'd taken the class, hauling out names I didn't know, repeating the praises they'd sung.

"Some writers take it more than once," she said, and "be sure to take it from Judy; someone else might teach it, but it won't be the same."

It all sounded a bit cultish to me, a bunch of writers flocking out to Brockport for an essay class. I wasn't sure I was ready for another classroom and the word *essay* conjured images of No. 2 pencils and blue examination booklets, so that it was perhaps the promise of the weekly drive more than anything that spurred me into signing up.

Judith Kitchen. A teacher who did not abide tardiness, lack of preparation, or prolonged deficiencies of imagination but who harbored certain soft spots for President Clinton, for Norman Maclean's novella of fly fishing, and all that's possible when words come together in just the right way. We read—did she assign Woolf, talk about Montaigne? I only recall my mouth hanging open while following a rumination on the color green by Marjorie Sandor and the feel of galaxies expanding while reading Albert Goldbarth's mash of religion, poetry, and physics. Essays. But nothing like the forced compositions of school days. More like the sun cracking open before sinking into Lake Erie.

From the French for making an attempt. *Essayer*. To try. Human thought winding its way toward understanding as it considers the words of a jump-rope song, a bride handing out favors on her wedding day, or the memory of a fourth-grade play that never quite fades. *Essay*. An entirely gorgeous word. Like the workings of human heart, but freer still. Wild and flapping. Capable of as much movement as a car headed west on the New York State Thruway, words becoming automobiles and airships and even shorebirds as they push forward and double back, hovering here and there, abrupt landings followed by august flights—each object, idea, and memory rising and, for a moment, held against the light.

I'd have taken it every semester if I could, Judith Kitchen's essay class. I'd made my way out of my marriage, had traded in questions about the approach of the age of thirty for questions about divorce, which I put forth to an attorney selected from the Yellow Pages—one whose eyeliner made a raccoon mask of her face and who kept her space heater blasting, even in July. A woman who looked to weigh less than the platform shoes that anchored her to the earth. She'd have blown away if not for those shoes. And being blown away had a certain appeal. I'd started taking the long way to class, driving along the Ontario lakeshore while listening to the classical station, the sound of bassoon mixing with the beat of wings. Watching gulls and herons take flight while trying to guess which category of drugs my divorce attorney was using—these were my pastimes, so I was primed, I suppose, for the movement of words on the page.

I would have been in her workshop again and again, until she denied me further entry or until the counselor I'd started seeing again intervened with warnings of obsessive compulsion or fixation, which would have been true; I was fixated. On this woman who opened worlds and handed them like new fruit to her students, on this form that made an art of an attempt—for what is life but a series of efforts?

And as it turned out no intervention was necessary; I took her essay workshop only twice before Judith Kitchen left western New York for the other side of the country.

That should be enough. A woman trading in the study of family systems and the remnants of a marriage for a word that means *to try*. It should be enough, and almost was. But as much as I wanted to take Judith Kitchen's writing class every night of the week and offer to carry her books and ask her feelings about adult adoption—in the end, it was Kitchen's writing more than anything that convinced me just how luminous an essay could be:

Days rise out of mist: my father transplanting the flowering quince; dandelions buttoning the lawn; my perch in the apricot tree, where white blossoms drop, like snow, in the breeze.

Days rising from mist. Blossoms dropping like snow. Beautiful and familiar.

I fall off the swing on the day of my Aunt Margaret's wedding. My new shoes slip on the polished seat and I fly, briefly, as though my heart, too, were lifted above the ordinary lawn.

Something unfolds as I read. I become a child again, rubbing my eyes, a kaleidoscope blooming behind my lids—a progression of color and shadow, peonies unfurling atop daisies atop roses, flowers opening like loosened fists, pink-fluttered parades of revelation.

How many times can you fly in a lifetime?

How many times can the heart detach itself?

I close the book and bring both hands to my face. The truth of it. Whether I sit or stand or race through time in a car going seventy miles an hour, this longing will remain. It will keep me company like the child I never had, pushing its way through the outlets of my body like the crocus does the hard earth—and why shouldn't it? What does the body know but want?

One life only.

A bird's flight, blue flicker from branch to branch.

What to do with such language? What to do but take it in a line at a time, stopping now and again for breath? What to do but swallow it whole, until saplings take root?

One for Sorrow

WHAT BROUGHT HER TO me the day the teacher played Mozart in music class?

It was only a recording; a serenade rising from the grooves of a code-laden compact disc, but she was as new as a spring flower, a first grader whose fine hair spilled into her face as she cried. "The music makes me sad," she said through wet fingers. And I was a counselor, so what could I do but peek under the pile of slippery hair and ask, "Did the music make you remember something?"

"No," she said, and I leaned forward, maybe even touched a shoulder. "What did the music make you think of? How are things at home?"

How inconsequential my questions. How little I knew compared to the girl. But I was a school employee, paid to ferret out the source of the girl's pain while she wept into strands of yellow hair until her breathing slowed and she could talk: "It's just so pretty," she said. "The music is very pretty."

✤

The next girl brought horses; how sturdy their backs, how golden their manes.

They were named for sweet things: Butterscotch, Miss Peachy, and Honey Pie. Her father read the Bible every chance he had, interrupting his scripture only to preach at his family for being so wrong. "My horses," she answered when I asked her to say more about home, "are the best friends ever."

Did I breathe a little easier when she brought out those horses, this child with a Bible-thumping daddy who sometimes let his snakeskin boots sink into her mother's side? I thought they'd lived in the subsidized apartments in the village where so many of the children who came to me lived, but no, this girl knew the feel of a horse, understood the possibilities of an open field. She talked on, dark hair smooth under the Alice band, a little adult as she told what she fed them, delighting us both with her horses, how she kept pictures of them taped over her bed. Until our time was up and I asked, "When will you ride them again, the horses?"

"Actually," she said, brown eyes going to the wall while the whole of her face became an exaggerated grin, "I was lying about the horses; I just wanted to talk about something nice."

What exquisite lies they tell, little girls. What perfect fictions.

If only you could press your ear to the wall and hear the silk of another girl who insists she can't remember her new brother's name because they'd stolen him just last week. She's scared her teacher with the story, bringing up kidnapping where other children bring up bedtime stories and new toys. "We took him when his mother wasn't looking," she giggles. "Mommy's been wanting a baby for a long time." She's five, a tiny thing—they are all tiny things, all round eyes and new hair—as she says, "Mommy stole him for us." So solid in her conviction, so thoroughly embarrassed over her failure to remember the pilfered child's name, there's no choice but to make calls to see if her mother has ever been pregnant and I must find what I'm looking for because the story stops there. But all these years later I still think of her; the fine cut of the lie, the way it continues to gleam as I look into it, part of me still believing that her baby brother came from the corner near the village gazebo like she said.

She lied too, Halladay.

With such certainty and stony face, there was no invitation to meet her in the land she'd created. Halladay's lies were like pebbles pelted at the world—lies to get others in trouble, lies to prolong her time out of gym class, lies to get an extra Tootsie Roll: "You promised you'd give me two!" Halladay was cemented by the rightness of her own lies as she stood before me, belly poking from under her sweater, bringing the legs of her pants above the ankles. A round belly for such a small body. One of the few swells of softness about the girl.

The blight of sorrow began that year.

I'd been warned about burnout in graduate school, and once I was hired in my first counseling position, I watched for it—waiting, I suppose, for all those sad stories to worm their way into my heart. But I'd worked with older kids and tougher kids and had heard so many hard stories that I thought I was immune. But no. My heart worked fine, it turns out, and flapped open when I least expected, in a bright school with construction paper fishes decorating the halls. It took years to arrive, but when it came, the sorrow, it arrived in one gigantic wave.

The verb "to sorrow" comes from the Middle English *sorwen*, the Old English *sorgian*; cognate with Old High German *sorgôn*. But sorrow has been with us long before Middle English or any English, before the human condition was parceled into nouns and verbs, from the moment the heart leapt like a fish inside the first human chest.

When tented together, Halladay's hands made a perfect church of flesh.

Brighter than her years, she'd skipped a grade, and was younger and smaller than the other girls, her hands still dimpled. She offered them to me once, her hands, when she found out I'd written a book. Even in the third grade she was an intellectual and preferred to speak of the writing of books than shows on TV. She liked cooking too and told of the dishes she might one day make and the exotic ingredients she'd need—an artist and snob at such a tender age. Most adults disappointed her, except for the original pair, who as they do for all children, became everything. Except for them, Halladay had no use for grown-ups, so easy to see through, so unaware of what she saw. But a book. Well, she'd heard about it and asked to read it. She'd read *Twilight* last year, so she thought she could handle it. Instead of answering, I distracted her with my need for a cover image—someone had suggested a child's hands and while the idea was not great, trying to shoot that cover was the most enthusiasm I'd ever seen Halladay express, almost smiling as she let me zoom in on her hands, the scratch of red nail polish flaking from the tip of each little nail.

A different child, this one with only one hand. She had two, really, but one stayed at her side, fingers locked together. The child had many fortunes. She was sent to school with a well-stocked lunchbox, wore a new dress nearly every week, had sprays of dark curls and eyes like the sea. So gorgeous a child you hardly noticed the hand, but it was there.

She came to me once a week for years. At first she was an elf, charming with her smile, hiding under my desk when I stepped into the hall. Then she read books and made regular reports on *Sweet Valley High*. Next she grew into a healthy rebellion and challenged me to games of Chinese checkers. Sometimes she asked me to open her milk carton or bag of chips, but only when the door to my office was closed.

We both understood that she'd been sent because of the hand and the way it made her feel; and though she was a beautiful girl with many fine dresses, she felt the weight of that hand—felt it so keenly she could barely speak of it. I was supposed to help her deal with her feelings, to help her see the beauty beyond the broken thing, even to find the beauty *within* the broken thing; and sometimes we could and sometimes we did, but she was a whiz, this girl, and saw what the world does with broken things. And so I spent my time in collusion, allowing a place where she could talk of the goings on at Sweet Valley, an office bright with posters and potted plants, a place to forget the press of the world outside its doors for a time.

Halladay rarely allowed herself displays of joy, but was incapable of pretense where sorrow was concerned. She cried over the stuffed raccoon she wanted to take from my office after every visit. She howled over the girls who wore matching leopard-trimmed skirts and would not let her sit with them at lunch. She crossed her arms and pushed out her bottom lip as she talked of her mother who swore she would visit this weekend—though her mother had problems of her own to deal with and was not able to come the last time nor the time before.

Another girl. All sun. Cascade of yellow hair, California face, this girl could not sit still. Butterfly. Hummingbird. Busy bee. Perfect except for the glasses perched on her nose that enlarged her already wide eyes so that catching her at certain angles made her face into nothing but eyes. She came because she liked to cut paper and I had good supplies—you can't imagine how much children will talk while cutting paper. This girl preferred the sort of scissors that turned the edges of paper into lace.

Her inability to be still was only a liability at school. At home it kept her awake until her mother passed out, so she could check to be sure she was still breathing and that the man who'd landed by her side at least looked kind. Sometimes the child's energy kept her awake enough to get in the car with her mom to watch the swerve of road. They'd landed in a ditch once and another time a man died in their apartment—something to do with drugs—but at least her mother was alive, her beautiful trembling mother. The girl never once complained. She just cut paper with scalloped edges and spoke of watching her mother the way other children talked about tracking the electric blue movements of their betta fish.

There's nothing like the way girls look at their mothers.

How they hang on every word. Nothing is lost on them. Nothing is wasted. The way her mother folds her arms when the girl begins to tell about her day. The way her mother looks out the window when the girl asks about her father. The way her mother taps her cigarette into the overturned wine cap to let down the ashes. Each and every movement. Her mother is a perfect dance, the sweetest ballet—all the feather steps, pirouettes, and fish dives a girl must study in preparation for the world.

Halladay came to me more than the others.

People warned me about the overly smart girl and her circumstances before she'd set foot in the school. She was one of the few to be sent to counseling twice a week and would have been sent more if she could. She could be nasty. She sometimes refused to cooperate in the classroom. She could not believe anyone liked her. The child who'd learned too early the maneuvers required to survive her particular circumstances. Only the gladness over her coming baby sister was unguarded. Wide smiles, easy laughs. What they were going to name her, where she would sleep. That baby sister. There were other times, I suppose—rare but not impossible—when she'd trip up and show her age, laughing without caution, letting herself push into me for a hug.

Then came one of the mothers, slow as sap, big as a tree.

The woman moved around in such drugged motions that her image was somehow as hard to lock onto as if she'd been quick. Her words came sluiced between thick lips, her eyes sequestered under lids so fleshy they barely opened. But she wanted the best for her kids. That's what she said, and other than the sad mountain of facts that was her life, I had no reason to doubt it. She showed she wanted the best when she complained about the food baskets I'd delivered, asking, "Why couldn't y'all get us a ham instead of turkey?" It was Thanksgiving and local food pantries doled out turkeys like Jesus doled out fishes and loaves. She was sick to death of turkey and her lack of gratitude at least showed signs of life.

In fact, when it came to making demands she could be downright energetic, coming in with a list of her daughters' sizes, having no shame about milking the school community, who in her mind were rich people, those with good haircuts and health benefits, people who talked about 401ks and things she knew nothing about. What she most needed couldn't be donated anyway and the children had their own troubles. If their backwoods accents didn't give them away, their ill-fitting clothes did. And they were, both of them, so very big. Baby Paul Bunyans. Replicas of their swollen mother. How the other children moved away. How the teachers tittered, even while offering up cans of sweet potatoes and new winter coats. There was no stereotype of poverty the girls did not embody—the abusive stepfather, bouts of drinking and work release, the broken-down pick up, all that and more. And yet the youngest child had a certain quality. Something about the smile hanging crooked on her oversized face, the light that came from it, as if she held the sun like a lozenge under her tongue. How fully it shone, that light. She'd learn to work it later—to shut down parts of herself to get through another move, another stepfather's hands—but back then, the child was simply and inexplicably the brightest light in the eastern Great Lakes.

So many hard-luck cases. So many mommas with bad boyfriends, so many daddies in jail. And yet in a school building with over a thousand children, most of them were like New Year's Day. Open, curious, seeking out sun. *Look what I made. Ten days until my birthday. I love you.* The age-old song of girls and boys:

One for sorrow, two for mirth;
Three for a wedding, four for birth;
Five for silver, six for gold;
Seven for a secret not to be told.

I indulge myself, hauling them out here.

But then they've always been here, swinging their feet, just waiting for me to look again in their direction. And though the sight of her hands clasped over her belly pains me, sorrow is no excuse to leave Halladay sitting for so long, a scowl of impatience taking up the better part of her face.

Is anything quite so withering as the scowl of a nine-year-old girl?

They are not quick to disapprove, but when they do, you know it. Except for the few rare girls deprived of fashion for religious or economic limitations, nobody understands beauty like a third-grade girl. She'll look you over from head to toe, taking in the bulky sweater, the plain pants, the outdoor boots. If she's bold, she'll say, "Why not change into heels when you're inside?"

They will love you anyway, because they are children after all, but most girls learn by the first grade that women are the bearers of beauty in the world and hope against hope that each one will bring them something new. They will stroke your hair when it shines, touch your earrings when they dangle, and offer up smiles when you remember to pack your heels and wear them inside, even—and especially—when it snows.

One of them made a close study of beauty.

Blue eyes and dark skin, hair that fell in glossy waves. Stunning in second grade, by fourth she'd learned to stop eating. Her chin might have seemed too sharp were it not for eyes that grew even larger in the hollow face—Disney eyes, big inky pupils nearly masking the irises.

She tended toward cruelty, and my time with her involved attempts to distract her from the gossip at which she was supremely adept. How sad, you will think, that terribly thin child already so cold, and I thought so too, and still do, except for the day I stood in the bridal shop in a deep lavender gown, one that had looked so good on the display model—one I'd hoped might be dusky enough for the evening wedding I'd arranged, but for which I'd waited too long to find a dress. A circle of mirrors enfolded me, casting so many reflections that I could no longer see. When I finally looked up from the folds of chiffon, there she was seated on a silk pouf chair.

We smiled to see each other outside of school and my wearing a dress the color of smoke. "I'm trying to find a last-minute dress," I said, and she didn't blink at the fact that I was getting married—she'd been bridesmaid to her mother already. Marriages come and go. She knew this and showed neither surprise nor delight. She just looked at the dress and shook her head, eyes rolling, tooth tugging a lower lip. *No*, the look said, *that will not do*. I tried another—white, this time, thinking she'd be taken in by the expected color for brides, but once again, she shook her head no. I was beginning to feel desperate, I'd waited too long and now nothing worked.

Try another, she said and her aunt shouted from the changing room to ask who she was talking to. *My counselor from school*, she said, and thank God the third gown, the color of raw silk, brought a smile to her face. That smile, so capable of cutting but also incapable of lying, meant everything just then. How I needed that exquisitely cruel child to save me when I needed to know something of beauty.

They all saved me.

Waves from buses, pushing their book bags into my lap to show the grades they'd gotten on their math tests, stopping by to tell about the dog having puppies. Just looking into their faces, just hearing the plans they had for the weekend and the simplicity of their needs (a hug, a song, a game) was the best part of many days.

Some of them are gone.

You come to expect the occasional tragedy with a parent—the slow mother collapsing in the street, never to snarl over the contents of a food basket again; the father arrested, put away for the best part of a child's life. Sometimes though, the girl herself is gone. Illness or worse; then it's a different matter entirely.

Sorrow, wilt thou rule my blood,
Be sometimes lovely like a bride,
And put thy harsher moods aside,
If thou wilt have me wise and good.

—ALFRED, LORD TENNYSON

Halladay's gone.

The girl who came to me two days a week, sometimes more, sliding her soft belly into a chair and asking to play hangman instead of talking about how she's treating friends. Sometimes managing little truths that she quickly took back and counted as lies. *Can I bring the stuffed raccoon home?* Yes, I said, and a few more meetings and a hug goodbye and that was the end of things for me. My final year. The mounting sorrow and the business of schools, the little hands posed for a book's cover—these things sealed the deal and I left. The years passed, but even five states away I recognized the face when it flashed on my computer screen last fall. Halladay and her new sister. Their father. A gun. The children killed near an Adirondack lake before their father turned the gun on himself.

There's more.

What she wore, the weather that day. Those hands, chipped red polish, pants barely covering the tender slope of belly. Autumn in the

Adirondacks. The smell of leaves and wood smoke coming from the cabins nearby, the sound of ducks overhead. There's more, of course, there's more. And sometimes I allow myself to think of it. For what is sorrow but the underside of beauty, the long-suffering cousin of joy?

❦

Now it's time for a boy.

So many girls—but they came to me too, the boys. The same stories, told in different ways. Now comes a boy. See his legs grown long this past winter. Notice the teeth, so white and straight for a sixth grader. His last year of elementary school. He has been sick, but after two visits to the school nurse, she calls me up and I walk over to the row of narrow beds and pull back the curtain to his padded cot.

"Where does it hurt?" I ask, and he says his stomach, a kind of heat, and maybe higher too, in his chest. He hides his face. All I have to say is, "I'd like to hear more about it," and the tears come and off we go to my office, where he lets it out. The girl, the tall one with a kind smile, the way he sees her in the cafeteria, the way he becomes knotted inside so that he thinks he must be very sick, that surely he will die.

"You like this girl?" I ask. "Yes," he says, *yes, yes.*

It's like a gift to explain love to a sixth-grade boy, to promise he's not dying so much as coming into another way of living. Lovesick. Something like bees swarming his gut. He's still pink when he leaves my office, but letting himself believe he will live after all. It will hurt to look at her across the length of cafeteria table, it will hurt to see the brightness of her eyes, but yes, he thinks he will stand up and try once again. Brave and brilliant boy. I close the door as he leaves, letting my head down on the surface of the desk. I put my head down, in the little office, and let it rest.

Brick House

I

When I first met my sister's father, I asked what he'd seen in my mother all those years before. "She was built," he said, and I produced a smile that pretended comfort with such talk. His honesty was refreshing, I suppose, and what had I expected him to say? They'd met at a bar, so it wasn't likely her politics or the perfection of her handwriting that had snared him.

"Stacked," he added, as if I hadn't quite understood the reference to the body my mother had, at different points in her life, shared with both of us. I changed the subject, spewing off a nervous stream of trivia about why some pistachios are dyed red and others aren't or asking how old he was when he started playing drums. It's clear to me now that nothing good can ever come from asking someone about his attraction to your mother, but then I could not help myself.

There were seven children in my family, with nearly as many fathers, and I was forever scraping together clues about how my mother had fashioned so many from just one body. The most basic questions are often the most stunning, and to me, our creations were as astounding as God's making Adam by emptying his breath into a pile of dust.

I had little trouble comparing my mother to God in heaven, but *stacked*? As in a brick house? The song went off in my head. Like any child of the '70s, I'd moved my body to the Commodores' hit, memorizing their grunted praises; and though my mother had been open regarding her sexual history—I was my own best evidence that she had no problem attracting men—seeing her as a fixed object was impossible. As the ocean, maybe. As the sky, perhaps, but never a house. Even if it were insisted upon and my mother obliged, flattening herself into four walls and allowing a ceiling to cap off her head—even then, the structure would be rough hewn and temporary; a lean-to along a mountain trail, a teepee fashioned of wild grape vines, a canopy of cattails and purple loosestrife.

II

How foolish of those pigs to build houses of straw and stick. We all knew it. Even as preschoolers we shook our heads at their lack of foresight. Nothing like a bunch of wayward pigs to turn four-year-olds into a clutch of hens, screwing our faces when the person reading the story came to the part about sticks and straw, the deliciousness of knowing where it would all lead—*I'll huff and I'll puff and blow your house down!*

Depending on the version of the story or the humor of the teller, the outcome was either a pile of bacon sandwiches or a series of pigs skittering off to the brother who'd taken the time to build his house right. The books must have been well illustrated because the image is lodged forever in my head; the relief on the faces of the straw and stick pigs as they find refuge inside brick walls, the straight back of the brick-building pig, a slight smile of superiority settling upon his snout.

We all wanted brick houses, we four-year-olds hearing that story. We understood about wolves, either from personal experience or from fairy tales. The point of the story seemed less about danger than the importance of proper planning and industry. I noticed most of all the way two reckless pigs were saved by the more diligent third, so that the story of the three pigs was also a primer in the necessity of identifying the bricklayer in any group. But whether it made us into builders or seekers, the story held out another promise. It said that security *was* possible, despite the various wolves that came calling. If only we built our houses with care, or found another who could, we'd be all right.

As if life could be held at bay by a wall of brick. As if anything were more solid than the running of the wind over a meadow of goldenrod in late August.

III

There was a woman, a lawyer appointed by the court, who came to the elementary school where I worked to check on certain kids. The few children unlucky enough to need court-appointed advocates were made luckier by their placement in her caseload. She had buzzed hair and wore a wide leather belt. She was solid as a house, this woman—a brick house, but not in the way the Commodores meant. Hers was a body built not so much for a man as for the care and keeping of others.

If she was depressed by checking on children whose families had blown apart, she never showed it. The sad stories, the mothers with empty bottles and flying fists, the fathers with loud voices and unflinching blue eyes, they were nothing more than frightened children in the face of this woman. A wall of a woman, she was. And before she left my office, she'd hand over a business card, saying, "Call if anything comes up." I knew she meant I should call if the child she'd come to see had a need, but what I heard was that I should call if any child who'd ever existed might need support—as if with her capable hands she could not only realign the off-kilter planets of our lives but hold them in place as well.

Whenever she walked into the counseling office, I thought of gunslingers from old Westerns and Samson before Delilah and other heroes both televised and biblical, in whose strength I'd never allowed myself to believe. But in her, I believed. She could hold the planets in alignment, this woman. She could shake the grit from the night sky and keep the stars properly dusted. And though it's too much to put on any one person, the tending of the universe, and though I left the school on my own that year and made my way into a different life, there were days when she arrived and I had to keep myself from grabbing hold of her wide belt, letting her pull me away from the cool façade of the school building, and skidding off in whichever direction brick houses travel.

Klotilde's Cake

SHE WAS A NEIGHBOR in Tucson, back when my in-laws lived there with their children, including my new husband when he was a boy. How long-limbed and brown he appears in photographs of their Arizona days, and how much of a retroactive crush I've developed on the ten-year old who learned to love the desert after a spring rain. Forty years have come and gone and still he speaks of the crimson tips of flowering ocotillo, the ocean of poppies, the blue lupine, and owl's clover. But nothing is said of the sadness blossoming in their neighbor. Except when my mother-in-law bakes the cake—the one the neighbor taught her to make, the confection named for her, at least at their house—and tells Klotilde's story as it is cut and served, the feelings at the table spiraling as we bite into its rum-dark layers.

It's the story of a husband leaving, returning to the place from which they'd come, Budapest or Prague, a place of statue-lined bridges and gilded spires thrown about like wedding cakes, which brings us back to Klotilde and the cake my mother-in-law serves as she remembers the woman, her voice pulling against the strings of the story. And oh, the loneliness of whipped cream, the anguish of broken eggs, the heartache of sugar folded into flour. It's there, the despondency of baked goods, if only one consents to notice.

My mother-in-law has eyes like the blue of Dutch pottery and sits quiet while we eat the cake. When I make naïve statements suggesting that perhaps things were not as bad as they seemed for Klotilde—

maybe her husband came back or she met someone new or took up a meaningful hobby, eventually forgetting him altogether—my mother-in-law only shakes her head. "No," she says. "No." She doesn't humor me, does not take hold of the branch extended by offering even a half-hearted *maybe so*. This I notice, because more than anything, my mother-in-law refuses to be deflated.

She rises early and walks fast before making breakfast and heading off to stand on corners with signs demanding rights for hotel workers and fair wages for the tomato growers of Florida, or to remind people on their way to soccer practice and shopping trips that we are at war and war kills; then drives home to work with her husband on letters to the editor about health care reform or runs off to read stories to kindergarteners whose families have no books before stopping to visit a friend in a nursing home, to drop a birthday gift for the man whose family has died or moved away. The two of them, my parents-in-law, nearly eighty now, think nothing of loading trucks with medical supplies for Cuba from the launch pad of their backyard. When they hear of hardship or injustice, their first response is action, which I notice and admire because I'm the sort to sit around eating cake while replaying secondhand stories and wondering what they might mean. Not so with my mother-in-law, who is out of her seat and grabbing a jacket; off to help a friend from Sudan; off to work at the overnight shelter for street people; off to register voters in Erie, Pennsylvania; off to deliver the cap she cap for a new baby— off to do more in one day than I manage in a good week. Still and all, around this one story, around this one woman, there is a slump.

But I have not yet said how it tastes, Klotilde's cake. If I say it is rich with warm overtones, you will not know. If I say that there's the slightest suggestion of coffee, that it inhabits the space between wistful and brooding, that the cake itself might be more rightly called a torte—still I will not have said enough. The cake is a woman looking over her shoulder as she boards a one-way train. It's the scratch of an old record, the words of a song you almost remember, the month of November as it gathers into a final sigh and gives itself over to December.

It's a wisp of a story, really, of the sort that's been told time and again; only the minor details vary—a woman abandoned to the desert, her husband flown off to the golden domes of home. She's young and there's a child who will never know the man gone away, so that as we eat the cake, I can almost hear a lullaby, the voice all loam and gut, the words in Czech or Hungarian or Romanian—or all them perhaps—because, in truth, Klotilde is nothing so much as the scent of vanilla and the froth of beaten eggs. And more than Klotilde, it's my mother-in-law who's caught me—this woman who does daily battle with the world, with energy left over for reading to school-children and baking cakes—the way she shakes her head and refuses to be soothed about a neighbor from four decades prior, denying me the lie of a happy ending, that makes me take notice.

Still, it's a delicious cake and my mother-in-law is a splendid baker, so I lift my fork for another bite, savoring all that is known, while absorbing—at least for the moment—all that can't be made right. We make our way through the icing into layers of sugar and rum and salt. The way they come together. The way each is needed. All of this, as I take up another forkful and let Klotilde's cake fall dark and sweet into my mouth.

Mock Orange

JUNE, AND THE SEASON for mock orange is upon us. It grows by the garage out back, a gangly shrub breaking into blossom, hiding the places where the wood has begun to rot. The flowers are like cream whipped by an overzealous hand, tossed about in sprays, falling from arched branches. Thank God for the mock orange, which allows me to look out the window and into the rain that does not stop.

I'm pregnant, her email said, and something caved in on me then, a heart or a lung collapsing in the space of time it took to read the message, changing for an instant my ability to breathe. In another instant, the message seemed like glass, or else I became glass. Either way, something was suddenly hard and clear and my niece's pregnancy became nothing more than a sound I'd been listening for since the baby shower I threw for her mother seventeen years before.

An immediate response can help to hide certain collapses, so I emailed back right away to show that I did not judge, that I still cared, that I was not hollowed out. I wrote a few well-intentioned words—*sounds hard* and *you are such a special person*—threadbare words, but no less true for overuse. Becoming pregnant at sixteen *does* sound hard, and she *is* special. She is, in fact, the most beautiful girl in the world.

Will it rise off her still, that quality which seems so much like confidence but is simpler, a grace certain people are born with—something in the face that makes others notice, something in her manner, quiet but full, that draws people in—will it still be there? If you passed her in your car—maybe she's laughing with a group of friends, maybe she's waiting for a bus on Lake Avenue, or sitting alone on a porch with broken front steps—would you see the light coming from her or would she be to you just another pregnant girl in the city, belly looming like the moon over her tiny feet?

What will I see when I visit? Will I be funny, my humor making little shelters in which to hide? Will I swing by Donuts Delite on my way, bring a box of sugar and flour as balm? I cannot know how it will go, because I have not yet brought myself to see her. And so this is the moment suspended. The space between imagination and reality. I hold myself here for as long as possible because it's delicious, this not knowing, though it exacts its price. I delay scheduling a time to see her until I can delay no more and set the date for Sunday, two days from now.

Years ago a cashier said how much my niece resembled me. It was Christmastime and she was four or five then, my youngest sister's child. She wore a winter coat trimmed in faux fur, her shiny black shoes making her look like a tiny present. Her hair was a mess under the hood, I remember, but even with the tangled hair, she lit up the children's department, eyes touching down on walls and shoppers and racks of ruffled dresses.

"You two look just alike," said the girl as she put our things into a bag.

My niece rewarded the clerk with a flash of eyes—she was always a little speck of something, flirting with the world before she could even walk—while I searched the beaming child's face. People often mistook her for mine but only because she was at my side as I bought child-size mittens and school supplies or signed her up for gymnastics class. No one had ever suggested we look alike. The same round face, of course, the same full mouth. But my sister's father is Iroquois and her husband is Puerto Rican, so my niece is Native American and Hispanic and a vague European mix—a dark-eyed girl who looks nothing like the pale-skinned aunt at her side. Still I remember the cashier's words that Christmas, her little coat, the uncombed hair, and all of it seems to me now a gift.

Mock Orange is named for orange trees that grow in Florida groves, whose blossoms perfume the air each spring. The mock orange is not a real orange though; it is not even a proper tree and does not produce any usable fruit. The shrub is largely ornamental, valued primarily for the way it mimics the orange's delicate scent. Yet even among mock oranges, there is great variety, some offering such sweetness you could close your eyes and imagine yourself among flowering trees after a spring rain, while others are so weak their perfume is nothing more than a wish.

See her at the art gallery in Philadelphia, standing before a panel of Tiffany glass, jewel tones swirling behind her, scarlet and gold, and the way—even with all the color—she outshines the panel of glass. Here she is as a three-year-old in Vermont, extending her hand to touch a cow. Now she's a five-year-old in a swingy dress at the hippie festival in Ithaca, a tie-dyed kerchief crowning her head. Now she's in my lap in a horse-drawn carriage trotting along the beach in Maine, the one with the boardwalk and the Ferris wheel, where the French-Canadians come. Here she is wearing her cat mask, refusing to speak to anyone in the entire state of South Carolina, offering only meows to waitresses and hotel clerks. Now she's at the aquarium, insisting on touching the stingray, taking in all the fishes, pressing her fingers against the glass, though I have told her time and again not to. A girl of two and five and twelve, laughing and crying and falling asleep in my arms—a girl who, despite it all, I've never been quite able to hold.

A colleague once asked if I sponsored a kid from one of those Save the Children organizations. I followed his stare to a photograph on my desk, one in which her oversized eyes look especially dark. Those eyes hanging open and her tan skin were the source of his confusion, and I knew him well enough to shame him but just shook my head at how wrong he had it—because when I think of give and take and what it means to love, I would say that for as long as I've known her, she has been sponsoring me.

She is mine, and I am hers. Bound by the fact that her mother was pregnant at a time when I was pregnant myself. I lost the child I'd hoped for, but my sister's baby was healthy and she named her for me. A daughter. One I believe my little sister has done her very best to share.

Her mother is the youngest in our troubled family. Left on her own at twelve, my sister waded through foster care and group homes into drugs and street life, and was eventually caught up in cross fire. I was the family member notified the night she was shot. My older sister is the strong one, but the people who notify families of tragedies did not know such things and somehow found me. I raced to the emergency room, the air electric, my sister's body a trembling mass, papers to sign, a pile of cheap jewelry handed over, someone asking whether I wanted to see a chaplain and what religion. I don't remember the priest or what words were said. Only the image of the tarnished jewelry has stayed with me, the feel of the metal cold and wet in my hand.

The bullet went clean through, as if her skin were butter. But skin is not butter—except in the face of bullets and sometimes love—and anyway, I tell you this not to create pity or to heighten the drama, but for context. Before my niece came into the world, there was her mother struggling with pain of her own and before her, another mother with her own set of injuries. Generations of wounds gone untended. So many shots fired, so much skin like butter.

People will sometimes ask, "When did you know you were no longer poor?" They ask because I seem to have transcended a childhood spent in poverty, which indicates a certain distance between myself and the thing transcended, a certain analytical tackling made possible only by removal from the stimulus—a certain precision, let's say. But I am not precise. I am not removed. I am only lucky in some things and unlucky in others. As to the question of when I was no longer poor, I sometimes believe poverty ended the day I realized I could go to restaurants as often as I wished or buy the shoes I wanted without waiting, or the moment I had access to an automatic icemaker—the magic of the machine, all those frozen cubes at the touch of a hand; I have never felt so rich. But now my niece, a brilliant and beautiful child, is pregnant and while the baby itself is not poverty (how could a child ever be?) the fact of his coming is—the tradition of longing and babies and incomplete mothering. No, a baby is not poverty, but early pregnancy and dropping out of school is, and the fact that I am not surprised. How I feel myself growing older as I write these words. That I knew and could only watch it unfold. That is poverty.

Grant me, then, this moment. Allow me talk of moonlight and flowers; let me make of this moment whatever works to bring her, while I can still can, as a child to my side.

She was gay for awhile, this girl so very much like the sun tilting into morning, you could not help but swoon. We were driving from Santa

Fe to Tucson, then north to Phoenix and Flagstaff and back again. She was thirteen, her phone an extension of her body. She chatted to friends back home while I took in the landscape, begging her out of the car to see the meteor crater, the Petrified Forest, to pose near a rusted-out car in the desert. Always she obliged, stepping out of the car, dark hair pulled back—and have I said, about the hair, how it contains the slightest trace of chestnut? But most of the time she was on the phone, and even when we stopped to meet a friend in Truth or Consequences, she refused to join us in the hot springs, choosing instead to soak in her phone. It was in that quirky desert town that she spent all her money on a ring with an opal set into the silver, a ring too large for her hand.

"For a friend," she said when I asked, her mouth so full of secrets her lips could not help but bloom—even when she was a toddler, she was never really a child.

"That's generous," I said. "But don't you want something for yourself?"

"No," she said. "She's a good friend, my best friend."

She told me in Tucson over brunch that the ring was for her sweetheart.

"I'm sorta gay," she said. We both laughed, she for how funny it sounded and I because I couldn't be happier. A gay niece suited me fine. A gay niece might defy the odds and graduate from her urban high school, where fewer than half of the students make it through. A gay niece might not have the burden of pregnancy added to an already heavy load.

"Okay," I said. "I'm happy for your gayness."

She talked about how it was hard to tell some people, and the conversation was serious for a turn, but then the French toast came and she told me about the girl she loved. Celina, it turns out, a girl named for the moon.

More than three years have passed since we were at Truth or Consequences. The desert, the hot springs, the ill-fitting ring—all ages ago.

It's raining now, and the sound is soft but unending against the surface of things. It is not pretty, this rain. The leaves on the maple out back have become so glossy they hardly seem real. I woke early this morning and now it's evening and still the rain does not stop.

"Maybe we should sit down with her—talk straight about her options," My older sister is standing in her mudroom, husband at her side; both have worried looks as talk turns to our niece.

"I think she knows her choices," I say.

My sister seems surprised. "Could a pregnant teenager really know her options?"

She's a mother and I'm not, but I have to wonder aloud where she grew up. "What girl in the city doesn't have every teacher, social worker, and doctor warning her about pregnancy? Do any of them not know about birth control, safe sex, and abortion?"

"But she may not know *all* the options," she says gently, as if I am missing something, and I think we're talking about adoption now.

"I'm sure she knows them, Steph." When she doesn't look convinced, I try another tactic. "At the very least, she would have seen the movie *Juno*."

In the movie *Juno*, an unusually well-adjusted high school girl becomes pregnant and spends her time hobbling around under the weight of a growing belly, forsaking junk food and continuing to attend high school. The girl manages to marvel at and care for her unborn child, yet give it away because she understands that they'll both be better off. The character is so captivating; it's tempting to think that my niece, who is a movie buff, will have admired her enough to consider the hard love of giving up a child. But only it's a film, a fiction, and even the smartest pregnant teen I've met is less certain about her place in the world than such a character, her unborn babies anchoring her to solid ground for the first time in her life.

What can be said of a shrub that bears no serviceable fruit? Is flowering enough? And where is the sense in a blossom named for the sweetest fragrance but that sometimes has no scent?

Juno is named for the Roman goddess. Wife to Jupiter, the goddess had no shortage of causes for jealousy and spite, but in her manifestation as Lucina, Juno was said to help ease the pain of childbirth. In the ancient world, women and girls ripped the braids from their hair as they labored, loosening their clothes and calling out to the Juno Lucina for help. The name *Lucina* is thought to come from the Latin word for light because a newborn was said to have been "brought to light" with Juno's intercession—but isn't it equally possible that Juno was called *Lucina* for the way she helped provide the world with new light, for what baby does not shine brighter than the sun itself?

My niece's parents don't seem upset. Divorced now, they're planning to throw separate baby showers. I think of birthday parties delayed over the years, or missed altogether because there was no money, no follow-through. I think of the *quinceañeras* my niece attended for other girls, cousins and friends, the one she'd wanted for her own, all the big talk about dresses and favors and venues—but in the end their lives were too much about survival to allow for party dresses and invitations. Not getting what you want, and not believing you ever will—this is the tradition we come from. But now a shower. We are pretty good at baby showers. Everyone playing games, a pile of presents, the easy familiarity of babies.

She will not give the baby away. And why should she, when it is the truest thing she's ever seen rise from herself in this world?

"It's tough." My husband doesn't really know what to say. He thinks maybe I should cry. "If she'd been raised in another place, if she'd had even just a bit more of a solid footing, think of what she might have done," I say. Of course, she can and will still do many things with her, but I can't quite see that now and while it's not a funeral, the feeling is there, the mourning and his trying to be kind because kindness is the best one can offer when one does not understand.

There are no guarantees in any family, of course, and such things as illness or despair can appear anywhere—but about certain facts, such as the completion of high school and avoidance of teen pregnancy, background makes all the difference and his nieces will not miss a step. It's not my husband's fault that his family is so intact; it has, after generations, only recently seen its first divorce. He can't help the stable home, the doctor father, and good schools. And why should he? Isn't that exactly what I'd choose for her if I could? So much is dumb luck; why should those born into fortune bear any blame for burdens not handed down? They don't. Of course, they don't. Such are my thoughts as I think of my girl and look out the window and can find nothing more to say.

The thing about the rain is that eventually it must let up.

Even now it has tapered a bit, and when I look out the window there are still the maple leaves almost plastic from the sheen, yes, but there is also the mock orange tumbling onto the garage, a rush of petals weighing the branches, as if richer for the weather. I do not say that the mock orange requires so much rain to be lush. I do not pretend that mock oranges in yards with less rain are as not as full or as grand, I only say that you notice it more when the rain goes on for so long. You notice such things, and what is there to do but run through the rain to take in the branches? Even when there is no fruit, even when the perfume is hidden—there is still the shock of blossoms, and what can you do but give thanks?

What I will say when I see her? I fear my judgment will show and is anything more corrosive than judgment? Or perhaps I'll go to the other extreme, loading her up with diapers and teething rings and celebrating this event in a way that says I endorse her choice—if it is a choice, because when you're sixteen, what in God's name is choice?

The most I can I hope for is to love in a way that neither holds back nor says that this is the best thing she will ever do.

And will you think less of me when I say that, in this moment, I cannot know if my grief is entirely about this child making another? In this moment, as a woman in her forties without children who has taken a sprig of mock orange into her hands, no longer expecting scent but marveling instead over the flowers, I must admit that I hear the sound of another bell ringing—something that knows better but keeps chiming anyway, saying that yes, this is perhaps the best thing she will ever do.

The Lonely Hunters

AL GREEN'S VERSION OF the song is over six and a half minutes long—just enough time to break you in two and put you back together again. Released by the Bee Gees in 1971 London, "How Can You Mend a Broken Heart" was brought home by Green in 1972 Memphis. The words become birds in Green's mouth, soaring, then spiraling in sudden downward flutters. And it's not the lyrics so much as the extended rises that matter, the calling out and all that's left unsaid that make Green's version the saddest song ever sung. So when he appears to Ally McBeal at the end of season two wearing a bow tie and singing this very song, how could I not feel my own throat go dry?

The human heart varies in weight from seven to fifteen ounces, and is usually no more than a pound. Yet even those few ounces sometimes feel like lead. An organ, yes. Flesh and blood, but more than that. The heart is the word we use to speak of the human core, the place where spirit and soul and feeling reside.

The ancient Egyptians believed the goddess Ma'at kept a scale with which to weigh the human heart. Upon death, the goddess plucked a feather from her headband, setting both heart and feather upon her scale. Only those hearts weighing exactly the same as the feather were allowed to continue their journeys toward the heavenly home of Osiris.

I didn't watch *Ally McBeal* when the show first aired. I tend to be about a decade behind on TV, watching *Seinfeld* long after it ended, cracking up about the Soup Nazi years after everyone else. Same with *Ally*. By the time I tuned into the quirky lawyer panicking over the dangers of not marrying by thirty, the character would have been well into her forties and most probably still single.

There's nothing better than snow and evenings of hunkering down in the early dark of new winter. Warm soup, thick bread, the scent of wood smoke. But as the season progresses, a feeling of containment comes like clockwork. No matter the many pleasant people or objects by my side, a mild madness descends, a sort of cabin fever, making me wish for wings. I settle instead for hobbies. One winter I decorated birdhouses, crafting nearly forty, each with a different theme—I attached white picket fencing to the Cape Cod and hot-glued Turkish coins to the one meant to represent travel. Another year I reread every single Nancy Drew mystery from childhood. Only when I began to develop a complex theory of gender politics based on Nancy and her chums did I finally give them up. I cultivated a grove of miniature orange trees for a few years, wringing my hands while waiting for the scented petals to come and cheat March of its gloom.

This year I gave up attempts at hobbies altogether; instead I took to bed in the early evenings, spending hours tucked away and watching episode upon episode of *Ally McBeal*.

The Heart Is a Lonely Hunter was written when Carson McCullers was twenty-three. She'd hopped a steamship in 1934, leaving Georgia for New York as soon as she could. Only seventeen, McCullers had already out dreamed her surroundings. In this way, McCullers is like Mick, the young girl in her novel who loves music so desperately she attempts to patch together a violin with parts from a smashed ukulele. The girl is so eager for strains of Beethoven that she burrows into the hedge near houses with radios and open windows, waiting hours sometimes for the music to come.

I should not have been surprised when Al Green appeared to Ally McBeal. I should have seen the soul singer coming a mile away. Ally had already been visited by apparitions of a dancing baby and was going through a rough patch, what with the mess she'd made with the handsome Dr. Butters and all. And the show had made a point of flexing its musical muscle, featuring guest spots by Barry White and Jennifer Holliday, as well as providing Ally with her very own group of backup singers—the Pips to her Gladys Knight, an imaginary trio swaying behind her, doo-wopping to every movement of her life.

Of course, Al Green woke Ally one night with his singing. Of course she stood, first in wonder, then crumpled into his arms for a slow drag around the bed. Of course. Al Green's rendition of "How Can You Mend a Broken Heart": Is there any better anthem to the gorgeous ache of living?

Back to Egypt, back to the goddess Ma'at with her feather and scale. While the purest hearts were allowed to continue toward the reeds growing along the Nile, those hearts found too heavy were fed to the soul-devouring creature called Ammit, or tossed into the fiery lake over which she presided. Either way, since ancient times, the heaviest of hearts have been fed upon by demons, while at their lightest, the heart can feel like a feather hovering toward a field of rushes.

Ally McBeal was a critical success, though some criticized the character's short hemlines, impractical footwear, and regular flights of fancy, declaring that Ally was not only an unprofessional and ill-informed representation of a Harvard-educated lawyer, but a gigantic step backward in the depiction of modern woman.

Exactly which television characters qualify as good role models for girls is unclear. Women still reign supreme on advertisements for cooking products and cleaning supplies, after all, appearing nearly ecstatic as they scrub floors and change diapers. Of course, men do laundry and cook supper, but not in the world of television advertising, where a woman engaging in self-indulgent rumination seems an improvement by comparison—or at the very least spares us the sight of a lawyer presoaking casserole dishes and shampooing the carpet before running off to a bail hearing.

The Heart Is a Lonely Hunter is nothing so much as a sad sweet song. More than anything else in the novel, more than the mutes or the doctor or any of the other lonesome characters, I'm taken in by Mick and her desire for music. The sound of harmonicas rises from back porches in the sagging mill town, and we're told that as a baby, Mick was calmed by her Daddy singing "Dixie" while beating out a tune against the coal scuttle. But the girl's head is stuffed with symphonies. Despite her lack of instrument. Despite the slump of the town under the Georgia sun and the weight of their days, leaving them too tired to think of anything as fruitless or vital as beauty. Despite all that, music buds within her.

Al Green turned from the limelight to gospel music in the mid-1970s—an unexpected move for someone who'd risen so far from Forrest City, Arkansas, a place strung with cotton fields and a federal prison, a town that calls itself the *Jewel of the Delta*. One of ten kids and the son of a sharecropper, Green had made good with a series of number-one hits, helping to solidify the sound of American soul music.

The story goes that the singer experienced a religious transformation after a girlfriend scalded him with hot grits. She seems to have been lovesick, and Green refused to marry her. That his most recent album had hit big with a track called "Let's Get Married" must have added to the sting—as did his bringing home another woman. After burning him with the pan of steaming grits, it's said that she found Green's gun and turned it on herself, leaving a note declaring her love.

She'd been beautiful, with kids and a husband in New Jersey, but the world remembers her mainly as the one who burned Al Green with grits, a woman gone mad with longing, the person whose death sent Al Green back to Jesus.

In my favorite episode, Ally's law firm defends a man who sees a unicorn. A bond trader, he's been fired for the insanity of his claim—how can people trust their portfolios to a man with full-blown hallucinations? Aside from all the unicorn talk, the man seems fine, and what is faith anyway but belief in the unseen? And we know a secret. Ally has seen one too, as a child.

"People who see them share some of the unicorn's traits—they're lonely, with virtuous hearts," the bond trader says.

The man, though fired, is gleeful and delighted to have been singled out for unicorn visitation. By episode's end, the unicorn appears once again to Ally. Fiction, of course, but even a cynic can hold her breath as Ally approaches the majestic creature that has materialized in her downtown law office. Even the most hardened of viewers, one who knows she's being manipulated but looks into those horse eyes, warm and dark, remembers that she too once loved unicorns.

I want—I want—I want—was all that she could think about—but just what this real want was she did not know.

—CARSON MCCULLERS, *The Heart Is a Lonely Hunter*

After a few episodes of Al Green apparitions, Ally's therapist, played by Betty White, tires of hearing her client whine about her relationship woes and musical hallucinations and finally succeeds in getting Prozac into Ally's hands. An episode-long philosophical struggle ensues, culminating in Ally's decision to flush the psychotropic pills down the toilet. She will not surrender her inner Al Green, she decides, nor the music that only she can hear. She's plagued by invisible music but chooses to believe in the power of the dream— one she did not summon and that costs her greatly but is so radiant she cannot flee.

I watched every show, even after things went south in season three (a senior partner becoming obsessed by the wattle of Janet Reno's neck, lawyers dancing to Barry White in the unisex bathroom, and Jon Bon Jovi as Ally's plumber)—crazy piled upon crazy, I kept watching. Because for all the make believe, for all the Betty White as drug-pushing therapist, for all the dancing babies symbolizing biological clocks and the strange and labored sexual fixations, ultimately, Ally's aloneness was pulsing and unabated and the truest thing I'd ever seen on TV.

> *Green wind from the green-gold branches, what is the song*
>   *you bring?*
> *What are all songs for me, now, who no more care to sing?*
> *Deep in the heart of Summer, sweet is life to me still,*
> *But my heart is a lonely hunter that hunts on a lonely hill . . .*

—FIONA MACLEOD, *"The Lonely Hunter"*

The title of McCullers's novel was taken from "The Lonely Hunter," a poem written by Fiona MacLeod in 1896. Fiona MacLeod, it was discovered upon death, was actually William Sharp, a Scottish writer who'd assumed the feminine pseudonym for the writing of his romantic poetry. Some say he adopted the Fiona persona to keep his scholarly reputation unsullied by sentimental verse, while others believe that he fell so hard for a woman he could not have that writing love poems as Fiona was the best way he knew to be near her.

It's so strong in some, the voice. To Carson McCullers, the gift was given. And to Fiona MacLeod and William Sharp. To the television character Ally, not so much the voice as the ability to recognize it when a good one comes along. Al Green's voice seems to have always been there. Before striking out on his own he'd been part of the family gospel act, but was given the boot when his father found him listening to the secular sounds of Wilson Pickett. But whether the young man sang gospel or soul, the voice was there.

It's still there, at the Full Gospel Tabernacle down near the Mississippi state line, where he rouses congregants with his *Yes, Jesus,* and *Thank you, Lord.* But it's only when, in midsentence, he breaks into song—*then sings my soul my Savior God to Thee*—it's only then, the choir coming in—*how great Thou art*—as everything moves upward, the Reverend Green's voice going low and ragged then rising, expanding, the choir pouring themselves out, something like a hard ringing of bells, that the hearts of those present for a moment take flight.

If I were a writer for *Ally McBeal,* I would not have ended the series by surprising Ally with a daughter from a botched egg donation a decade prior. I would not have allowed the eccentric senior partner to evolve into a mariachi singer at a local Mexican restaurant. More than anything, I would have not let "To Sir with Love" be Al Green's swan song from the show. It's a fine song, and it was touching to see Al and Ally dancing down the streets of Boston, the lampposts strung with fairy lights, both characters smiling as Al trails off into a swirl of stardust. If only he could have stayed a bit longer. He might have fixed a decent meal for Ally, who'd grown thin over the years—a plate of collards and pork ribs. He might have sung some more about the heart, his and hers and ours. They might have headed down to Memphis, where they'd scratch their names on the bricks outside Graceland while Al tells Ally about Stax and Hi Records and the sounds of the city back in the day. They'd head toward the Mississippi, following the bends of the river before hopping a trolley to an evening of southern fried and Beale Street.

I have tried to fill my heart with honey, which is not as silly as it sounds, given the way the liquid shimmers, the slow soak of it into each of the cells. I've succeeded with gin or brandy and sometimes love. Some use the pages of their Bibles to set papier mâché casts over the heart, while others survive on celery sticks or a Mozart sonata or by memorizing a certain turn of verse by Edna St. Vincent Millay. Some allow themselves the impossibility of unicorns; others reread books from childhood or follow the sound of Al Green as he stomps his feet and shouts praises that flare without warning into love songs.

Despite all this talk of feathers and goddesses and bittersweet songs, it's not the heart I speak of. Not really. The Italian word for gypsy, *zingaro*, is perhaps a better word. *Heart* is merely a convenience, a sort of shorthand for what's contained within the cautious body—the spark that thrives on wonder, that which is flung wide or ratcheted shut until it seems all but sealed but remains open, if only just a touch; the thing that moves and changes even as we seek to know it, that which stalks and stalks but cannot be satisfied. Not fully. Not permanently. The part of us that continues to yearn, to try, and to dream, despite the fact that there's a certain space within us incapable of being filled, and that learning to live with this is a part of our humanity. But what does the heart know? *Zingaro cuore.* So great are some hungers, so unrelenting, that whatever even halfway fills them must be tried—miniature orange trees and birdhouses and homemade ukuleles. What can we do but feed, then feed again, the tender shoots within us?

Something Like Joy

YOU USUALLY GET HERE this early?" asks a woman, sixty or so, white uniform dress, stockings, white shoes, as she drops her clothes into an open machine.

"No," I say, "I've never been before noon."

"I love this place early," her voice is soft but strong, the accent more Mississippi than Arkansas, "before everyone else gets here with their big bags of clothes and children piled up all over the place."

I like the quiet too, the waiting while clothes spin and soak and dry, flipping through magazines and staring out into the parking lot, watching people come and go with their takeout boxes of BBQ, all of it in a sort of suspended animation—the Laundromat, where nothing is expected beyond feeding quarters to machines and scooping soap and softener at the appropriate times. But this morning is different. It's my birthday, though that's something no one else can see. No, the real difference is that I have plans while I wait. A tall coffee and a stack of student papers on the table near my basket.

"I just got off work," she says while letting the lid to the washing machine come down, "I work from six to ten every morning."

She works at the elementary school nearby, and says no when I ask if she's a nurse, smiling in a shy way that reminds me of Rose Middlebrooks from junior high, the friend I'd forgotten until this very moment, with eyes as brown and skin as golden as the woman standing at a washing machine thirty years later. "In the cafeteria," she says, "fixing breakfast."

I ask what she cooks and she says it's more like reheating frozen things than actual cooking and sometimes it's as simple as setting out donuts and boxed cereal and whatnot.

"Well," I say, "I'm sure the kids like all that stuff."

"Yes," she says, "they sure do." She sits beside me saying she notices I have only one load spinning in the washer and do I live alone. I nod while tucking the paper I'd been grading into my bag. "I have a husband, but he's away a lot," I say and realize just how sad it sounds. "And two cats," I tack on, as if it won't sound sadder.

I want to tell her about my husband's talent, the way he's home right now making a painting of the river, and that we'll go to the pub tonight for leek soup and soda bread and beer. And more than that, I want to explain that I don't mind the solitude, my love of space, the price of which is sometimes loneliness. I want to describe the way it settles around me, the space and the freedoms I have, the way my life has both worked out and not worked out according to anyone's idea of success. But she's only asked about my lack of laundry and is now telling about a cat she once had and her current menagerie: two parakeets and a betta fish. "I talk to them birds all day long," she says, laughing. "*All* day long, Lord."

"I hope you don't mind my asking," her voice changes, the laughter evaporating, "but why did you move here?" Her eyes go shy again and as I scan the smooth face, I think maybe she's not so old after all, or I am truly grown older today, the gap between us closing. Anyway, I'm used to this question and the tone in which it is asked. Unlike New York or San Francisco, where the appeal is generally assumed, Memphians are stumped about why outsiders come. The tourists down on Beale Street, the British and Germans lined up at Grace-land they almost understand, but someone coming to stay? It's nothing short of a mystery.

"A job," I say, and tell her about my students at the local public university, how I was the first in my family to go to college, how so many Memphis students are in the same boat. I like this woman who reheats frozen pancakes for a horde of hungry children every morning and

I suppose that besides technically answering her question, I'm hoping for something more, but she just looks away and asks if I know her niece over at the college.

"I'm afraid not," I say once she says the name. There are more than twenty thousand students, but I leave this out, not wanting to dilute her niece among the others.

I stand to check my laundry, asking if she takes naps after working all morning.

"Only after I watch my programs."

"Soap operas or game shows?"

"Neither," she says, "I like the old ones, *Bonanza*, sometimes *Gunsmoke* and *The Big Valley*. And *Walker, Texas Ranger*; now *that* is my show." I laugh at her taste for television Westerns and wonder if she likes old detective shows, like *Starsky & Hutch*.

"Not really," she says. "But I love that *Barnaby Jones*."

"What about *Quincy*?" She shakes her head, she doesn't know much about *Quincy*, and I'm spinning my wheels trying to remember shows from childhood when she switches to movies.

"Normally I don't care for Elvis, but I like *Frankie and Johnny* a whole lot," she says. She throws me a look of pity when I don't know the film, and says, "the one where Elvis is on a riverboat with the girl who played Elly May in *The Beverly Hillbillies*."

"What about other musicals?" I say, moving to the washer whose red light has finally gone dark. "*The Sound of Music*?"

"No," she laughs. "I don't like that kind of show."

"*West Side Story*?" I pull the wet ball of clothes into the metal basket as she asks what it's about and I say it's Natalie Wood as a Puerto Rican girl who loves a white boy but no one wants them together. We both laugh then—though I'm not sure whether we're laughing over the idea of Natalie Wood being Puerto Rican or the fact of people being kept apart by skin color.

"Hmm," she says after a minute. "I do like me some Shirley Temple films."

"Yes," I say, "she's all right," while slipping quarters into the dryer, and by the time I return to my seat the entertainment thread has worn down to nothing and it gets quiet, something settling onto us, the sort of thing that can't be turned back once it starts. As I sit listening to the clank in the spinning dryer, all talk of *Bonanza* and Elly May Clampett out of the way, I know the question she'll ask before it comes—one that didn't used to come, or when it did could still be answered with the sort of possibility that let both answerer and asker off the hook.

"No kids?"

"No," I say. "Nope."

It's odd the way the tender places are not touched so much by those we know as by strangers sitting in metal chairs while laundry tumbles behind small circles of glass. Funny how such moments come between talk of old TV shows and the sound of the man in the pick-up outside revving his engine while waiting for his girlfriend to switch her load.

"You never wanted any?" She's looking straight at me now, silver curls catching the light. I look away for a minute, toward the woman who runs the place, folding laundry for those who prefer to pay more and drop it off, her long hair pulled back in a utilitarian bun, a style she's probably worn for forty years, a habit as fixed as the way she apologies every time I ask for change, *yes, ma'am, sorry, ma'am,* while handing over the half roll of quarters.

"You really want to know?" I look back at the woman beside me, and a man who's just taken a seat at the table starts flipping through a magazine when she says, "Yes."

"I never could," I say. I feel something then, something with force enough to cause tears in the Laundromat but with muscle enough to stop them at the root. *No children. Never could.* The fact of it still so strange. Something's moving in me, and she's watching closely, and though some small part of me wants to apologize for no good reason, like the woman as she changes dollars into quarters—*no, ma'am, sorry, ma'am*—I say it clean and cool, as if I'm ordering a Diet Dr Pepper from the counter next door. "I tried and couldn't, then the marriage ended and now I'm older, married again and children wouldn't fit."

She keeps looking, our eyes almost connecting, the blue and the brown, before something flits away in her, and who knows, maybe I flit too from a moment so swollen it nearly splits, from this Laundromat stuck between a bowling alley and THREE LITTLE PIGS BBQ in southeast Memphis.

The man at the end of the table coughs and turns the page of the magazine and something loosens around us.

"How about you?" I ask, and listen as she tells about her boy, how his wife is expecting and how excited she is, but she hopes they don't think she's putting a crib up at her place. And it's a fine conversation then, her telling about her son while I get up and begin to fold my clothes into my basket.

"They sure don't look dry," she says after a minute, "You planning on air drying?"

"They're dryer than they seem," I say.

"Hmmm," she says. "Well, maybe you'll come in at this time again."

"Maybe I will," I say, and don't tell her how far from home this Laundromat is, how I traveled nearly twenty minutes from a neighborhood of big houses and fine streets to sit in this particular place, so far removed from anything familiar. I don't say it because I can't make sense of it myself, and realize just then that I'm ready to make my way home. I gather up my coffee and basket of damp clothes and the bag of ungraded papers, and say, "It was nice talking with you." I tell her my name and ask for hers, which is odd considering I'm on my way out the door.

"Joyelle," she says—or maybe the name is Joelle—either way it comes too fast, and all I know is that it sounds something like joy as I prop the door with a hip and push into my car fast because it's started to sprinkle. I put the basket in the backseat and sit for a minute watching the sun filter through bare oak branches and—not despite the rain, but because of it—the light is just right. To say the sky is washed in gold would be too much, but there are hints of it everywhere, yellow light coming through the crown of black branches, so that I feel the weight of the day just then, the perfectly full weight of it.

Coda

This River

AND JUST LIKE THAT autumn is here again. I've left behind apple
orchards and Great Lakes, exchanged cattails for catfish and the
muddy banks of the lower Mississippi—but the scent of fall hangs
in the air the same way everywhere. This morning I find a message
written upon a paved path near the river as I walk—words scrawled
in pastel chalk:

WE HAD OUR FIRST DATE HERE.

Sweet, I think. I walk a few more feet and find another:

RIGHT HERE, ALONG THIS RIVER.

The word *river* is underlined with two squiggly lines of blue, as
if making the symbol for water; the word *here* is capitalized as if to
mark the very spot. I keep walking, and the messages keep coming:

WE HELD HANDS.

Who is this writer sharing memories along the walkway? A barge
loaded with coal passes and a mockingbird calls from a cottonwood
tree. I continue along the path, wondering how many more messages
have been written. A few more and the path narrows. I find what will
be the last message—the letters are capitalized, and hearts chalked
in pink surround the words:

WHAT A GOOD FATHER YOU'LL MAKE THIS JULY.

I do the math. Newly pregnant, and sharing her news. A romantic,
this writer, walking him along the path of beginnings, revealing her
news a few words at a time. She may not have intended to announce

their pregnancy to those of us attempting to walk off breakfast or to center ourselves before heading to work, but here they are, her words:

RIGHT HERE.

When will the next rain come and wash them away?

And what can any of it mean, the invisible couple, the memory of a first date, this secondhand joy, all of it written in chalk?

ALONG THIS RIVER.

How such things press upon on us, I think, as I step over a swarm of chalk-drawn hearts, feeling excitement for the child coming in July. A child I will never know, but how glad I am of its coming. Strange to be suddenly connected to strangers through messages chalked on the walking path on Mud Island. But how much they mean, these words written upon the path, this handful of symbols that will disappear when the next hard rain comes. How much they matter, stories of apple trees and chipped vanities and holding hands along the river—the traces of our various backs and forths, our reaching and spinning, our many falls, and the occasional wondrous flights. All of it set down like white stones through the forest, like so many little glints of light.

A Thousand Thanks

To Kristen Elias Rowley and the University of Nebraska Press for shaping this book and for all they do to promote literary nonfiction. To Gregory Gerard, James Graves, Jenny Lloyd, Elizabeth Osta, Sally Parker, Deanna Ferguson, Jim Mott, and Maureen McGuire for careful readings. To my colleagues at the University of Memphis, my writing community from the University of New Orleans, and my students who mean more than they know. To Dinty W. Moore, Linda Allardt, Joseph and Amanda Boyden, and every writing teacher I've ever had (including Srs. Eileen Daly and Clare Ehmann, who kept me in line and taught me to diagram sentences, in that order).

To Gail and Peter Mott, Elizabeth Ross, Kristen Iversen, Richard Bausch, Marcia Aldrich, John Griswold. Deb Wolkenberg, Gia Lioi, Craig Bullock, Lisa Shillingburg, and friends, editors, and former colleagues who have so generously supported my work. To Toni Plummer, Valerie Sayers, Jennifer Warlick, Kathryn J. Thomas, Susan Latoski, Nancy Bennett, Darlene Cowles, Patricia Roth Schwartz, Beth Lathrop, Kathy Zawicki, Leigh Simone, Nina Mortellaro, Connie Boyd, Natalie Parker-Lawrence, Mary Louise McClelland, Beth Thomas, Minter Krotzer, Terra Keller, Betsy Hoffer, Kelly McQuain, Shelley Puhak, Kathleen Willis, Julia Walsh Postler, Leanne Charlesworth, MJ Iuppa, Mary Anne Parker-Hancock, Adam Lewandowski, Scott Gould, Mamie Morgan, Young Smith, Curt Nehring Bliss, Terry Forward, Roberta Liebhaber, Leanne Charlesworth, Phil Memmer, Kathy Pottetti, Martin Lammon, Carol Moldt, Deb Vanderbilt, Jen

Litt, Anne Panning, Sarah Freligh, and others who invited me into their classrooms and organizations.

To Ellen Wheeler and Mary Ellen Sweeney of the Susan B. Anthony House in Rochester, New York, for the tour, good information, and for putting up with silly questions.

To my family—Livingstons, Skyes, Rosarios, Heywoods, and Motts—who remain my primary way of knowing the world. To families and friends from Corpus Christi, especially those from the old neighborhood—who could have guessed that a dead-end street could stay in the heart so long?

To Jim Mott for knowing when pelicans will fly over Arkansas and where to best view the moonrise and how to find wild azaleas along trails that have become our own.

Source Acknowledgments

With much gratitude I acknowledge the journals in which earlier versions of these essays appeared: "Land of the Lost," *Arts & Letters*, no. 27 (Spring 2013); "Our Lady of the Lakes," *Bellingham Review*, no. 67 (Fall 2013); "World without End" and "Klotilde's Cake," *Blackbird* 13, no. 2 (Fall 2014); "Our Lady of the Roses," *Fourth Genre* 14, no. 1 (Spring 2012); "One for Sorrow," *The McNeese Review* 50 (2012); "Mock Orange," *Water~Stone Review* 17 (Fall 2014); "The Lonely Hunters," *Seneca Review* 41, no. 3 (Spring 2013); and "Something Like Joy," *River Teeth* 14, no. 2 (2013).

"Land of the Lost" won the 2012 Susan Atefat Prize for Nonfiction from Georgia State College, "Our Lady of the Roses" was listed as a Notable Essay in *The Best American* series (2013), and "Mock Orange" was a finalist for the 2014 Judith Kitchen Prize in Nonfiction.

Notes

THE LADY WITH THE ALLIGATOR PURSE

Information on the public poll comes from *New Dollar Coin: Public Prefers Statue of Liberty Over Sacagawea: Report to the Honorable Michael N. Castle, House of Representatives* (Washington DC: General Accounting Office, 1999).

Information on Susan B. Anthony's purse comes from the Susan B. Anthony House in Rochester, New York, and their website: www.susanbanthonyhouse.org.

"The Lady with the Alligator Purse" is an American hand-clapping song with many variations, including versions in which the mother is called Miss Lucy or Miss Suzie and the Lady sometimes utters "nonsense" or "nothing" to the child's problem. I combine the version I sang as a child with one recorded when Susan B. Anthony campaigned for suffrage in California.

Blackstone's Law was published as Sir William Blackstone, *Commentaries on the Laws of England* (Oxford: Clarendon Press, 1765–69).

FLIGHT

All italicized text comes from Judith Kitchen's essays "Songs to Undo the Spring" and "Only the Dance," in *Only the Dance* (Columbia: University of South Carolina Press, 1994).

ONE FOR SORROW

"One for Sorrow" is a traditional English nursery rhyme based on superstitions and the number of magpies one sees.

The verse from Tennyson is taken from *In Memoriam A.H.H.*, sec. LIX, 1849. From *In Memoriam* (Portland ME: Thomas B. Mosher, 1890).

THE LONELY HUNTERS

The line from Carson McCullers is taken from *The Heart Is a Lonely Hunter* (Boston: Houghton Mifflin, 1940).

The poem "The Lonely Hunter" was written by William Sharp and published under the pseudonym Fiona MacLeod in 1896 and appears in *From the Hills of Dream: Threnodies, Songs and Other Poems* (Portland ME: Thomas B. Mosher, 1901).

"How Can You Mend a Broken Heart" was written by the Bee Gees in 1970 and covered by Al Green in 1972. No actual lyrics appear in the essay.

EPIGRAPHS

I

The lines from "Persephone, Falling" are by Rita Dove, from *Mother Love* (New York: W. W Norton, 1996).

II

The lines of the anonymous Irish poem "Táim sínte ar do thuama" are taken from a translation by Frank O'Connor in *Love Poems of the Irish*, ed. Seán Lucy (Cork, Ireland: Mercier, 1967).

III

The lines from Judith Kitchen come from the essay "Songs to Undo the Spring," in *Only the Dance*.

To order or obtain more information on these or other University of Nebraska Press titles, visit nebraskapress.unl.edu.